"Get ready to meet a delightful asso~~~~ throughout the ages who will guide ~~~~~~~~ ~~~~~~~~~, purposeful steps toward a Jesus-centered, hope-filled life. This is a book you will go back to many times!"

—**The Most Rev. Michael B. Curry**, presiding bishop of The Episcopal Church; author of *Love Is the Way* and *Crazy Christians*

"What could be better than spending time with friends—including some spiritual masters—who give you insightful and enduring advice on how to live? Karen Wright Marsh's beautiful new book introduces readers to some of the women and men who have guided her along life's difficult but also delightful paths, helping her—and now us—find a way to wonder and joy."

—**James Martin, SJ**, author of *The Jesuit Guide*

"I was surprised by how much I needed the spiritual sustenance that *Wake Up to Wonder* offers. Marsh highlights the lives of familiar and new companions, ordinary people whose creativity and purpose radiate long after their earthly sojourn has come to an end. Then, she invites us to nurture our own wellsprings of wonder."

—**Barbara A. Holmes**, core faculty at the Center for Action and Contemplation; author of *Joy Unspeakable, Race and the Cosmos*, and *Crisis Contemplation*

"Both in print and in person, Karen Wright Marsh has been a friend of mine for years. Her presence in both places has helped to root my soul in a deeper awareness of meaning and purpose."

—**Jon Foreman**, front man for Grammy Award–winning rock band Switchfoot

"Karen Wright Marsh successfully combines the wisdom of spiritual masters with her own down-to-earth insights to provide an easily accessible toolkit for those who are seeking an antidote to the stress and chaos of the modern world. Her invitations to sing, breathe, walk, and so on give people simple ways to fill up the spiritual gas tank and face the challenges of life with renewed hope and strength."

—**Sister Monica Clare, CSJB**, TikTok influencer

# WAKE UP
## to WONDER

*Vintage Saints and Sinners:*
*25 Christians Who Transformed My Faith*

# WAKE UP to WONDER

### 22 Invitations to Amazement in the Everyday

## KAREN WRIGHT MARSH

**BrazosPress**

a division of Baker Publishing Group
Grand Rapids, Michigan

Published by Brazos Press
a division of Baker Publishing Group
Grand Rapids, Michigan
www.brazospress.com

Printed in the United States of America

Library of Congress Cataloging-in-Publication Data
Names: Marsh, Karen Wright, 1961– author.
Title: Wake up to wonder : 22 invitations to amazement in the everyday / Karen Wright Marsh.
Description: Grand Rapids, Michigan : Brazos Press, a division of Baker Publishing Group, [2023] | Includes bibliographical references.
Identifiers: LCCN 2022058983 | ISBN 9781587435805 (paperback) | ISBN 9781587436048 (casebound) | ISBN 9781493441884 (ebook) | ISBN 9781493441891 (pdf)
Subjects: LCSH: Christian biography. | Christians—Religious life. | Conduct of life—Biblical teaching.
Classification: LCC BR1700.3 .M373 2023 | DDC 270.092/2—dc23/eng/20230303
LC record available at https://lccn.loc.gov/2022058983

The opening epigraph is from "Miracle Fair," in Selected Poems of Wisława Szymborska. Translated by Joanna Trzeciak. New York: W. W. Norton, 2001.

The author is represented by C. Fletcher & Co.

The illustrations for this book were created by Annie Davidson and may not be reproduced without the artist's permission.

Baker Publishing Group publications use paper produced from sustainable forestry practices and post-consumer waste whenever possible.

23  24  25  26  27  28  29       7  6  5  4  3  2  1

For Charles,
who amazes me

*An additional miracle, as everything is additional:*
*the unthinkable*
*is thinkable.*

—Wisława Szymborska

# CONTENTS

## DWELL   149

# INVITATION TO WONDER

*Once upon a time,* I aspired to a successful, worthy life through spiritual regimens, diligent labors, "good choices"—all powered by a stubborn confidence in the future I presumed God had mapped out for me. Somewhere (Sunday school?) I'd gotten the idea that right belief, right intentions, and right discipline would deliver personal achievement, an adoring family, robust health, wealth, and the added bonus of inner equanimity. And so I sailed forth.

My oh my, have I ever been humbled.

Ambitious systems? Lofty goals? Assurances of a dogged faith have not held up as expected. I've been chastened by garden-variety heartbreak, the wear and tear of ordinary life, the messiness of trying to love actual people. Recent global events have brought me face-to-face with my human precarity and often drive me to fear and loneliness. Forces that are beyond my control—climate, politics, technology, economics, science, culture—overwhelm comprehension.

Still, I haven't given up on the spiritual life; in fact, I need a steady inner grounding more than ever. In my questing, I've come around to unexpected answers.

At some point, I had a revelation. It was nothing profound, really, but it caused a lasting change in me. I realized this: I do not need to find and follow the perfect *plan*. (What a relief!) What I truly need is *people* I can follow—older sisters, brothers, mentors, spiritual friends who have been this way before.

In my search for people over plans, I've found my way to faithful Christian women and men from across centuries and cultures, each with challenges all their own yet very much like mine. Their varied stories are thrilling, heartening, extreme, bizarre, even unremarkable. For all their flaws and eccentricities, they discover, or in some cases blunder into, a spirituality of amazement and encounter God's presence shimmering everywhere.

Afflicted by deep melancholy, the reformer Martin Luther found relief in singing. Cast out as an accursed Brahmin widow, India's Pandita Ramabai discovered dignity and purpose in the pages of the Bible. As a boy, Patrick of Ireland, that saint now celebrated with green beer and shamrocks, endured enslavement by a savage warlord yet returned to the place of his suffering out of compassion for the Irish people. Civil rights pastor-philosopher Howard Thurman suffered racism at the hands of white American Christians yet found deep rest in the liberating, loving religion of Jesus. The lifelong activist Dorothy Day cherished her escapes to the beach.

I've become a collector of stories and a curator of historical Christian practices reframed for the everyday, inspired by the host of ancient wisdom figures who mentor me in the ways of wholeness. In a world where "religion" is associated with burdensome dogma, judgmental attitudes, and blind faith, these persistent believers disarm with a spirituality of discovery, attention, even freedom.

You and I are in a fragile, unsettled moment, aren't we? You may have experienced inherited doctrine and a presumed religiosity that have failed to reach your tenderest places. Can we dare to imagine a new way of living now—to navigate the world with an empathy, kindness, and hope we've never known before?

This is what I long to share: the infusions of meaning, purpose, grace, attention, and amazement granted by the sinner-saints of the Christian faith whose enduring wisdom and words ground me every day.

I invite you to come along as I tell stories of the guides who show me the way, or rather, the multiplicity of ways, to live a centered, abundant life of prayer and action, insights and habits. They just may intrigue you too simply by being who they were and doing what they did.

I hope you'll dip into the personal practices and spiritual disciplines I offer as invitations. The invitations are borrowed from research reported by scientists, ancient habits and devotional traditions, methods advanced by mindfulness and wellness experts, beauty from poets, and plain old common sense from folks who live life well.

Guess what? Invitations are not rules; they are not systems! They are prompts, overtures, welcomes. So take all the freedom you want as you flip through this book. Read a story here, try out a prompt there, scribble a note, make a sketch, then take a nap. Read deeply if you like—or skip ahead and come back later.

As you make your way through, you're sure to meet generous, wise teachers who have glimpsed the transcendent. They notice the tiny quotidian miracles hidden right underfoot. They teach that life is a creative work in progress, a long-term project in which patience is required. They are saints of amazement who hold out fragments of the Life that is life. They beckon you too to "taste and see that the LORD is good" (Psalm 34:8).

This is life. Fragile. Surprising. Blessed. And you're invited.

*When I found I had crossed that line [to freedom], I looked at my hands to see if I was the same person. There was such a glory over everything; the sun came like gold through the trees, and over the fields, and I felt like I was in Heaven.*

—Harriet Tubman (1822–1913),
Scenes in the Life of Harriet Tubman

You and I inhabit a universe of extra-ordinary marvels both massive and miniature. So why the sense that I live life dimly and with a divided heart, passing by, unaware, the commonplace gifts that appear along the path? Why am I too distracted or fearful to experience the nourishment, the salvation, to be found in the crumbs of life?

*Presence* is what we are all hungering for, aren't we? Real presence! Could it be that you and I have simply never learned to be present with quality to God, to others, to ourselves, and to all created things?[1] To bring our attention to unfolding moments?

In the first portion of this book, you will meet five spiritual guides who, each in their own way, call us to wake up. *Wake up, wake up!* Tiny miracles are to be found everywhere, they say: in a bite of sun-ripened peach, the languorous stretch after a nap, the buzz of a melody, a deep cleansing breath, the self-revelation that emerges when a pen is put to paper. Look within and without and you just may encounter God, beside you in the world, in the glory over everything.

Pay attention. You stand on holy ground.

# PUT PEN TO PAPER

## HENRI J. M. NOUWEN (1932–1996)

*It was an early September Saturday,* the first day of Henri Nouwen's sabbatical. He sat down in the little apartment that would be his temporary home and cracked open a brand-new journal. Upon his arrival in Ontario that day, his hosts had invited Henri to "just relax" at the beginning of this "empty year." "Just sleep, eat, and do what you want to do," Hans and Margaret had said before leaving him to himself.[1]

Relax? That had never been Henri's style. Over his sixty-two years, Henri had been ordained as a Catholic priest; earned academic degrees; taught at Notre Dame, Yale, and Harvard; written more than forty books; traveled and preached; lived among the poor in South America; and served in communities of care where he lived alongside people with intellectual and developmental disabilities. Henri's close friends had long worried over the frenetic, emotionally intense eighteen-hour workdays that pushed him into episodes of nervous exhaustion and collapse. This time around they'd written him a no-nonsense letter, a "sabbatical mandate" ordering him to say no to all work except writing.

Now faced with an empty journal page, Henri admitted to a flood of feelings. "I am excited and anxious, hopeful and fearful, tired and full of desire to do a thousand things," his first journal entry reads. "I feel strange! Very happy and very scared at the same time. I have always dreamt about a whole year without appointments, meetings, lectures, travels, letters and phone calls, a year completely open to let something radically new happen. But can I do it?" he asks himself. "Can I let go of all the things that make me feel useful and significant? I realize that I am quite addicted to being busy and am experiencing a bit of withdrawal anxiety."[2]

Henri Nouwen followed a lifelong practice of personal writing. He made some volumes public: his accounts of months at a Trappist monastery, a sojourn through Bolivia and Peru, his participation in the L'Arche community. He kept a "secret" journal through a particularly dark, despairing, and lonely time. Thanks to his willingness to put his feelings on the page and his generosity in sharing them, we've received a rich legacy of recorded human experience. Nouwen's journal from this final sabbatical period is a gift to workaholics everywhere: one restless man's honest reckoning with his varied emotions. We read along as he rejoices in his new freedom yet has to nail himself to his chair whenever wild impulses drive him to get busy—busy with anything at all. We hear him admit that he is left without excuses and resigned "to embark on a new journey and to trust that all will be well."[3] Alone in his secluded room, Henri determines to fight with the angel of God and ask for a new blessing.[4]

Henri J. M. Nouwen was and is beloved around the world. With uncommon honesty, this self-identified "wounded healer" was open with his own brokenness, for he believed that his psychological wounds, physical limitations, and emotional needs could be a conduit of grace and healing. Pain was not something to be hidden away. "I am convinced that it is possible to live the wounds of the past not as gaping abysses that cannot be filled . . . but as gateways to new life."[5]

To his readers, Nouwen is a trustworthy guide through the shadows of self-rejection and into the daylight of God's love; he's a fellow pilgrim who could offer assurances like this: "You are facing a real spiritual battle. But do not be afraid. You are not alone. . . . Remember, you are held safe. You are loved. You are protected. You are in communion with God."[6] Over and over, Henri offers variations of the same glad message, the same good news: you and I are the beloved of God from eternity to eternity. This is who we are whether we feel it or not.

And so—in what would turn out to be his final year of life—Henri started his sabbatical days with breakfast and morning prayer, sometimes Eucharist with neighbors, and then he retreated to his third-floor apartment to write, a candle burning nearby. The entries in the beautiful cloth-bound journal, written in long hand, are confessional in classic Nouwen style. "My unconscious certainly has not gone on sabbatical yet!" he begins, in an account of chaotic dreams of missed meetings, angry people, and unanswered letters. Upon waking to a silent room, he can only laugh and pray, "Lord Jesus Christ, have mercy on me."[7]

He writes that his prayers, which he calls the bridge between his unconscious and conscious life, feel "dead as a rock."[8] What an extraordinary priest it is who can confess that, instead of being full of spiritual fire after all these years, he doesn't feel much of anything when he prays. And yet Nouwen responds to tumultuous emotions, tangled visions, and dry prayers with the inquisitiveness of an open heart. What are the darkness and the dryness about? What do they call me to? he wonders. "My wild, unruly dreams will probably keep reminding me of the great spiritual work ahead of me. But I trust that it is not just I who have to do the work. The Spirit of God joins my spirit and will guide me as I move into this blessed time."[9]

# TRUTH UNDER THE TAPE

I found the journal, with its brown leatherette cover and the words "My Diary" in gold script, in a box of stuff from middle school, under the Camp Sandy Cove photos, a broken locket, and faded report cards. My name is inscribed inside, a child's flourished attempt at elegant handwriting: Karen Elizabeth Wright. The first pages are filled with uninspired accounts of homework, a class field trip to the Crayola factory, a minor mishap at Sunday school, chicken for dinner, a Friday night watching *The Brady Bunch* at Barbara's house. Long before the thirty-one days of January are done, the entries trail off, nothing more than a phrase, maybe two. Rainy today. Social studies project due. Dog threw up.

Then I find a curious mound on the page for February 12: multiple layers of paper, each layer sealed down with tape, one on top of another. And on the top layer? The words "DO NOT OPEN. OR ELSE." Finally, something worth reading? I peel off one piece of the decades-old tape and then another until I'm three layers down. "I hate Dan Wright," I read. (Dan Wright being my younger brother, the second in our tribe of five kids.) Another scrap of paper, another piece of tape, and my writing, "I hate Daniel Burton Wright." Then "I hate DBW." "I hate Daniel B. Wright." Variations of his name multiply the force of my anger, an anger papered and taped over, a feeling so dangerous to my adolescent self that I'd been careful to seal it away from the eyes of any present or future reader who might come upon that little brown diary. A reader who would surely judge me should they ever know the rage in my young heart.

Frankly, I hesitate to recount this story, knowing that the very same Daniel Burton Wright will likely read this and learn that, as a sixth grader, I once fiercely hated him on a particular February afternoon. My twinge of shame points to just how far I still have to go in this journey toward vulnerability. The evidence is right there in yellowed paper and curling tape: the twelve-year-old me quite literally buried her bad, sad, guilty, and wrathful emotions, and the grown-up me does not find laying them bare so easy either.

How unlike that girl is Henri Nouwen, who was so very open about his shadow self—those parts of him that a more protected person (me) might deny or hide out of shame. By the time he was in his sixties, he knew that his private journal would be read some day, by friends and probably by thousands of strangers, and still he wrote sentences like these: "My whole being seemed to be invaded by fear. No peace, no rest, just plain fear: fear of mental breakdown, fear of living the wrong life." Nouwen writes of other feelings too: "It is a wonderful sensation. It is the sensation of belonging." He writes of hope: "I don't know how God is going to fulfill his promises, but I know that he will, and therefore I can . . . know and trust that the deepest desires of my being will be fulfilled."[10] Feelings, feelings, and more feelings, all over each page.

For careful people like me, Nouwen bravely shows the way toward exposing one's true emotions—to one's self, first of all. He teaches the restorative power of journaling, where anything and everything can come to the surface and into the light. More than a few times I've resolved to keep a daily written account, knowing in my head that it is a healthy practice, but I haven't followed through, citing the weak excuse that there's no safe place to hide a diary and my precious privacy from "curious" others.

Today I wonder, too, if I simply haven't felt comfortable with the experimentation, the messiness, the confusion of naming my struggles for myself, long before I've dared to speak them out before others. Henri doesn't judge. You have been wounded in many ways, Nouwen tells me, and your wounds are deep. "Many tears still need to be shed. But do not be afraid. The simple fact that you are more aware of your wounds shows that you have sufficient strength to face them."[11] I sense Henri next to me here in the solitude of my room as I turn to another entry in that old diary, as I unstick another fragment of tape, as I pick up a pen to write a new and braver page.

# TRY THIS

Ready to put pen to paper right now? Choose among these prompts or follow your own idea. There are no rules in this book!

## Get It Down

Journaling is one of the more effective acts of self-care and, happily, one of the cheapest. Naming emotions and acknowledging tough and traumatic events, as Nouwen did in his own journals, can have a demonstrably positive effect. Scientific studies have shown the cascading benefits of journaling, ranging from increased mindfulness, memory, and communication skills to better sleep, a stronger immune system, more self-confidence, and a higher IQ.[12]

Even a one-time fifteen- to thirty-minute session of focused journal writing has demonstrable advantages. Why not try it for yourself today? Aim for writing that is strictly stream of consciousness; just get your thoughts and feelings out onto the page, without worrying about your topic or whether it will all make sense.

These journal pages are not meant to be art or argument, and they are certainly not intended for anyone else. Write on paper or tap on your laptop. Channel a bit of Henri, who said, "I have promised [to write down], as honestly and directly as possible, what is happening within and around me."[13] After you've written freely, notice how you feel. Has anything shifted?

## Fill Your Emotional Toolbox

Many of us think of our emotions in primary colors—basic ones like happy, sad, angry, or surprised—if we think of them at all. But it can be useful to name our emotions with a bit more specificity and nuance. Identifying and differentiating our emotions is a skill, one we can practice and improve to the good of our overall emotional and mental health.[14]

Here's an exercise to get you thinking and writing as you put pen to paper. Brainstorm as many emotions as you can think of: negative, positive, and beyond. (There's an online list of 271 emotions if you need inspiration.)[15] I've written a few to get you started. Next time a feeling arises, stay curious and think of your list. Can you give your emotion its particular, nuanced name?

### Emotions List

| | | |
|---|---|---|
| Astonished | Alarmed | Apprehensive |
| Content | Distracted | Expectant |

## Dig Deeper

*Whatever I will "feel," it is important that I keep making inner choices of faithfulness . . . less dependent on fleeting emotions and more rooted in lasting commitments.*

—Henri J. M. Nouwen, Sabbatical Journey

Henri Nouwen was moved by powerful feelings, yet here he speaks to the importance of lasting commitments and practiced choices. (He also adds, "My body and soul might need an immense amount of discipline to catch up with this wisdom!"[16])

What is your own personal style? Your inner tendencies toward emotion, discipline, and commitment? Ask yourself:

- Can I think of a time when strong emotions got in the way of what I believe to be true about myself, others, or God?
- Can I think of a time when my discipline or commitments kept me from experiencing important feelings?
- Is there one "lasting commitment" that is especially important to me?
- Is there any "inner choice of faithfulness," however small, that I might enact today?

# SING OUT LOUD

## MARTIN LUTHER (1483–1546)

*Rev. Martin Luther gave out a great deal of advice,* much of it documented in his three thousand letters to parishioners, friends and family members, princes and commoners. Topping the pastor's "Don't" list: lying late abed, gluttony, harsh ascetism. On his "Do" list: gardening, hard work, bowling, Scripture reading, joking, games, wine, prayer. To Prince Joachim of Anhalt, a twenty-six-year-old afflicted by "melancholy and dejection of spirit," Martin urged the companionship of others along with the healthy rigors of riding and hunting—and warned him against a fear-based solitude that is "poisonous and fatal to all people, especially a young man."[1]

Six months later, when poor Joachim was no better, Martin prescribed music—singing and playing instruments—as the pathway to healing. Music, the absolute best of God's gifts, could "rule over the feelings of the human heart" to "make the sad joyful, the joyful sad, the timid brave and the proud humble."[2] Songs of God's mercy had the power to shield the prince's heart from evil and drive away Satan himself.

In his day, Martin Luther was an enthusiastic singer, capable lute player, passable songwriter, and prolific hymn writer who composed "sermons in sound." This church reformer and cultural influencer hosted choral parties at his house and filled every church service with song, urging even illiterate congregants to join in with the choir. "I, Dr. Martin Luther, wish all lovers of the unshackled art of music, grace and peace from God the Father and from our Lord Jesus Christ!" he pronounced.[3] Woe to any tactless person who dared assert they just couldn't or wouldn't sing, for they got a verbal thrashing from the doctor: he condemned them as bumbling idiots worthy to hear only the braying of asses and the grunting of hogs.[4] To be fully human was to sing: using this beautiful and priceless gift granted by God to praise our good Creator, experience fellowship with our sisters and brothers, and embody with our voices the beauty of life.[5]

Martin's elevation of music went far beyond his personal, artistic preferences. Singing had its subversive uses too.[6] Since the fateful day the young monk had posted his inflammatory Ninety-Five Theses on the Wittenberg church door, then refused to recant his radical disputations, the church in power had outlawed him as a heretic and banned his writings. But where books could not go, pop songs readily could. Martin Luther combined familiar German tunes with catchy, theological lyrics to broadcast the Reformation message of God's liberating grace.

Regardless of listeners' ability to read, their social standing, or even their location, the songs went viral; it was reported that husbands and wives, young women and men, literally *everyone* was soon "gladly singing" Martin's infectious songs—collapsing the old divides between the secular and the sacred, the domestic and the public, the here and now and the eternal.[7] In the town of Magdeburg, so many people loudly sang Luther's German psalms on repeat that hymn vendors were declared a public nuisance and imprisoned.[8]

As this new community made music together, they were converted into a lyrical culture of resistance, Scripture, and worship. "The Word of God should be read, sung, preached, written and set in poetry," Martin wrote. "Wherever it may be helpful and beneficial, I should gladly have it rung out by all bells and played on all organ pipes and proclaimed by everything that makes a sound."[9] Even the youngest children in their midst were schooled in music and raised in this theology of melody.

To the end of his life, Martin Luther heeded the counsel he had once given to gloomy Prince Joachim, for he too was afflicted by episodes of dark depression. Music brought healing to Martin's struggling spirit and assured him of the coming bliss of heaven, complete with angelic choirs. Music was a gift Martin returned to God with praise of his own, singing:

> For God our loving Lord did Music make
> To be a proper singer, the master of composers:
> Day and night she sings and sounds God's praise.
> Since nothing will tire her in praising the Lord,
> My own song, too, shall honor God
> And give God thanks eternally.[10]

# THE THING THAT HAPPENS WHEN WE SING

I'm out of breath when I reach the plain brick building with just two minutes to spare. I slip into my seat as the warm-up begins: scales, stretches, trills. It's been a hectic Monday: a morning mountain of emails on top of the backlog of tasks from last week, the unwelcome surprise of a broken dishwasher, no time for that workout I'd planned. My brain is still buzzing with worry as we open our scores to Rachmaninoff's *All Night Vigil*, the liturgical Orthodox worship service written as uninterrupted, unaccompanied choral song.

Around me sit an accountant, an English teacher, an astronomer, a dog walker, a freelance writer, an ER doctor, a professor. But for the next two hours, only these distinctions matter: soprano, alto, tenor, baritone, bass. Michael, our director, calls us, the members of the Oratorio Society of Virginia, to begin with movement nine, "Blagosloven esi, Gospodi." As I reach for the notes of the first alto line, aim to breathe in the appointed places, stumble over the unfamiliar Church Slavonic (I should have practiced), and try to keep my eyes on Michael's direction, the fret of Monday falls away. I am all attention, all body, all breath, all presence. We start and stop, break down the lines of chant, fix that B-natural for a B-flat, tune a high note, sing a tricky section yet another time, refine some pronunciation; this piece will take over an hour to sing from start to finish. We work, week after week, toward that moment when all fifteen movements will shimmer with the resurrection, as they surely must have on the Moscow night in 1915 when Rachmaninoff's masterwork was sung for the first time.

Being like this with other people brings a particular satisfaction. All that we will produce, in the end, is a seventy-five-minute concert after months of Mondays in the drab Municipal Arts Center building, yet we will have done it in company. We watch, listen, and breathe together; as we do this, scientists report that our hearts literally beat in unison as well. Choral singing strengthens feelings of cooperation and well-being, reduces stress and depression, increases life expectancy, and improves symptoms of Parkinson's and lung diseases. That calming mindfulness we feel when we sing? It comes thanks to a boost of oxytocin, the hormone that helps control anxiety.

What a relief to let our concerns settle, to feel our bodies take up space, to sing in a language either familiar or strange, to be alongside someone else, without words even. How healing it is, too, when on other days we head out alone to take a hike, ascend a rocky slope, finally catching our breath at the summit to take in the view, and, just maybe, sing out loud into the open sky.

# TRY THIS

Not quite ready to join the choir? Follow one or two of these invitations instead.

### Tune In, Rock Out

You may not play the lute, compose songs, or sing in a pleasant tenor voice as Martin Luther did, but don't let that stop you from feeling the rush that comes from music. There are many ways to make today a lyrical day.

- Go ahead: sing in the shower.
- Search playlists for music that meets you where your spirit is right now—or takes your feelings where you'd like them to be.
- Put in some earbuds, turn up the volume, and play the childhood tunes you loved best. (Think middle school.)
- Take your soundtrack out on an invigorating walk, moving with the rhythm.
- Grab a friend or family member to share, sing, laugh along with you. Karaoke, anyone?
- Don't resist the urge to dance!

Take a cue from the Bible's King David, who owned up to his exuberant dancing in this way: "In GOD's presence I'll dance all I want! He chose me . . . and made me prince over GOD's people, over Israel. Oh yes, I'll dance to GOD's glory—more recklessly even than this" (2 Samuel 6:21–22 The Message).

## Sing to Learn

A saying attributed to playwright and poet Alfred Mercier states that whatever we learn with pleasure, we never forget. Listening to and performing music activate areas of the brain associated with memory, reasoning, speech, emotion, and reward. Music helps us not just retrieve stored memories but also lay down new memories, regardless of our age, development, or musical ability.[11] Intuiting that singing enhances learning and memorization, Martin harnessed music to teach people Scripture and doctrine. Use that power for your own growth:

- Choose a Scripture verse, psalm, or poem that you'd like to learn.
- Do an online search and you're likely to find it set to music somewhere (try YouTube or Spotify).
- Need an idea? There are countless online playlists of Scripture for memorization.
- Once you've found a version you like, listen to the song three times through.
- Write down the words for yourself, bringing your complete attention to the text.
- Now listen to the song again, exercising your memory to reach for the words; you might even sing along.
- Repeat until you know the passage by heart.

## Welcome the Earworm

"There's a song stuck in my head!" It's a common and sometimes annoying experience. Martin Luther would say you've got an *Ohrwurm*, or "earworm": a brief segment of music that automatically comes into your awareness and keeps playing on repeat. Nearly everyone experiences earworms; this is our brain's inheritance from preliterate times, across all cultures, when music and rhyming helped us hold on to oral stories and information.[12]

If there's a musical phrase from a pop song or commercial ditty that afflicts you, why not channel its power by substituting a snippet of words you'd actually *like* to remember? A Bible verse, line of poetry, phrase of affirmation, or math formula? And what if you started singing your new composition out loud? It might even get into other people's ears too!

# FOLLOW YOUR BREATH

## THOMAS MERTON (1915-1968)

*Thomas Merton threw himself into the religious life,* but he made it all seem natural—as natural as breathing. "What I wear is pants. What I do is live. How I pray is breathe," he mused in a 1965 essay.[1] Out in the forest, he felt the Word blow through the trees, and he breathed it in, inhaling God with his whole body, soul, and spirit. "My God," he said, "I pray to you better by breathing. I pray to you better by walking than by talking."[2]

Once a despairing, faithless university student who'd been converted—much to his own surprise—to a wholehearted Christianity, Thomas traveled to the quiet Kentucky woods to devote himself to a life of contemplation in God and for God. Tom, as he was called by his friends, was ever a man of the physical world who burst with energy, moving in a flow of breathing, striding, and conversing. Some have described him as a man who leaned into paradox: a humble person who enjoyed fame, a Catholic priest fascinated by Zen Buddhism, a solitary mystic who craved company, and a cloistered monk who died far from home.[3] He was also the celebrity author of sixty books and the most popular Catholic writer of the twentieth century.

Thomas Merton's many readers followed his insights on current politics, culture, poetry, justice, and, most of all, the spiritual life. Tom's message was simple: each and every one of us is invited to encounter a God who loves, chooses, and visits us. Contemplation of the sacred is not reserved for intensely religious people but is available to all. God is as near as our next inhalation.

In his advice to those longing to experience God, Tom begins with the scriptural admonition to "pray without ceasing." What does this mean? "It is really quite simple," Merton explains. "It is just as if Our Lord told us, 'You must keep on breathing, or else you will die.' The only difference is this: breathing is instinctive, prayer is not."[4] Yet prayer is as vital for the life of the soul as breathing is for the life of the body. That is why Merton gives this encouragement from Luke's Gospel: we "should always pray and not give up" (18:1).

Tom's descriptions of prayer are embodied as well, evoking *ruach*, the ancient Hebrew word for spirit, breath, wind: the very breath of God that creates and sustains all things. Since the beginning of humanity, the Old Testament teaches, we who breathe with the *ruach* of God are blessed to participate in the flowing gift of life.

Drawn to the promise that prayer can be as simple as respiration, as sustaining as oxygen to our lungs, we follow Thomas Merton back into the pine grove, to the simple cinder block hermitage in a forested area of Gethsemani Monastery, where he lived and prayed and wrote his books and letters.

Surrounded by trees, those "all sufficient exclamations of silence," one can imagine him getting up from a rustic altar, where he's been praying on his knees, to work, "cutting wood, clearing ground, cutting grass, cooking soup, drinking fruit juice, sweating, washing, making fire, smelling smoke, sweeping, etc. *This is religion*," he declares. "The further one gets away from this, the more one sinks in the mud of words and gestures."[5]

As he went about his daily rounds of work and prayer, Tom the Christian considered the spirituality of his Buddhist friends, Zen monks whose meditative breath practices brought them to contemplate the present moment amidst ordinary life. Despite the doctrinal differences between them, the spiritual brothers aspired to leave human mediators of religion behind, stand still, breathe in, breathe out, and stand on sacred ground.

Tom Merton invites the many of us who dwell in "the mud of words and gestures," who are baffled by faith but would like to pray, to do this one thing: step outside. "About prayer," he begins, "have you a garden or somewhere that you can walk in, by yourself? Take half an hour, or fifteen minutes a day and just walk up and down among the flower beds." Don't try to think about anything in particular. When distracting thoughts come to you, don't try to push them out by force but see if you can let your mind relax; you may find that God's will is revealed to you through those very thoughts. As you walk along, you are, in fact, *already* praying "because our Lord is with you."[6] And remember, everywhere and always, to breathe.

## INHALE. EXHALE.

It took me a while to get comfortable with the breathing thing. At a spiritual wellness retreat years ago, I sat with the other participants in the light-filled cedar lodge. "Close your eyes. Drop into your body," the seminar leader said quietly, lighting candles at the center of our circle. "Become aware of your breath. In and out. In and out." Legs crossed, suddenly self-conscious, I felt tightness in my throat, a pain in my chest, breaths becoming shallow, threatening to end if I ceased following the exhale and inhale, a labor suddenly dependent on my mind. The more I thought about this involuntary physical action, this thing I'd done since birth, the more anxious I became. In and out and in and out and in and out. How long could I keep it up? I slipped out of the lodge, into the blazing Wyoming sunshine, and hiked up the rocky trail to the ridge, stumbling, panting, desperate to release all that *intention.*

Since the failed attempt at wilderness meditation, I've leaned toward more vigorous wellness pursuits, often with earbuds supplying podcasts, audiobooks, and playlists to occupy my buzzing brain. I've run, walked, danced, worked out on elliptical and bike machines, lifted weights (okay, only for about a week), and dismissed swimming altogether. One Saturday a few years ago, a friend invited me to a vinyasa yoga class. I was lured in by her promise of coffee and croissants afterward. I felt queasy and awkward on the mat, toppled over a few times, but I went back. Again and again.

Following the teacher as we moved through the poses required all my concentration; each movement was synchronized to one breath. Between the inhales, crescent lunges, exhales, shoulder stands, and planks, there was just no mental space for to-do lists or rehashing last night's tense exchange. For the first time since Wyoming, each inhale and exhale became an anchor, taking me somewhere I wanted to go, to the next place in the flow, and on to the blessed relaxation at the end of the class. Yoga is a part of my routine now, the only thing that will pull me out of bed before sunrise. By the end of each vinyasa class, I find that I've been breathing deeply with intention but free of the self-conscious worry that once arose in stillness.

Breathing is vitally important, as every living creature knows (except for one nonbreathing, ocean-dwelling, jellyfish-like parasitic blob). The oxygen we draw in through respiration is necessary for life itself. Good thing our bodies have taken care of that, no thought needed, ever since God formed the first human out of some dirt from the ground, blew the breath of life into the body's nostrils, and made the human come alive—a living soul (see Genesis 2:7).

Both vinyasa and Thomas Merton have taught me that breathing can be so much more than an unconscious bodily function. It can embody God's creative power that first uttered the world into existence and filled humanity and all animals with life. Breathing is a rhythm of inhaling God's perpetual gift of vitality, of exhaling devotion, creativity, love, and mercy. Whether I'm walking to work, folding laundry, reconciling expenses on a spreadsheet, picking up a screaming toddler, teaching a class, or showing up on a yoga mat, I am, of course, breathing—and if Tom is right, I am praying too, and our Lord is with me.

## TRY THIS

Breathe easy! There's no pressure to do all these exercises. They are offered solely in the spirit of experimentation.

### Why Breathe?

The Latin word *spiritus* can mean breath, breathing, breeze, or air. All religious traditions teach that breathing is more than a physical requirement to live; it's foundational to our spiritual, mental, and emotional well-being. Hindus call it *prana*; in Chinese medicine it is referred to as *chi*. As a Christian, I believe that the Holy Spirit breathes in me—that same *Ruach Elohim* of the Hebrew Bible who created and sustains the world.

Our breath is a powerful tool that readily offers most of us an easy way to help us manage stress and anxiety. The physiological effect of deepening the inhale and lengthening the exhale acts on our autonomic nervous system to shift us out of the body's fight-or-flight mode and can interact with both cognitive and physiological aspects of anxiety. Breathing exercises offer scientifically proven benefits to cardiorespiratory function, metabolic health, improved relaxation, and sleep.[7]

- What is your own experience of conscious breathing?
- What feelings and thoughts come up when you begin to concentrate on your inhale and exhale?
- Take a moment to write your response.

## Breathe the Box

Breathing exercises are convenient because they can be practiced anytime, anywhere, and without any equipment or teacher. Box breathing, or square breathing, is a very simple exercise that has been shown to reduce stress and boost focus and concentration. Here's how you do it:

- Breathe in through the nose for a count of four.
- Hold the breath for a count of four.
- Breathe out slowly for a count of four.
- Hold for another count of four.

As you repeat the steps, imagine that you are making a square or box with your breath.[8]

## Five-Four-Three-Two-One

If breathing exercises just aren't for you, here's another way to bring your thoughts to the present moment. Use the following prompts to become aware of your surroundings. Take all the time you like.

What are *five* things that you see?
What are *four* things that you hear?
What are *three* things that you feel?
What are *two* things that you smell?
What is *one* thing that you taste?[9]

Enjoy deep, leisurely inhalations to ground yourself in this sensation-filled moment.

### Choose Your Own Adventure

The internet abounds with articles, videos, and resources on the why and how of breathing, some more science-based than others. What appeals most to you? Look for breathing exercises and try one or two, bookmark some for later. You might even practice along with a vinyasa yoga video or attend an in-person class (and reward yourself with a pastry).

### Breathe with the Breath of God

Highlight or underline the words or phrases in the following passage that hold meaning for you right now.

> Through [God's grace and Holy Spirit] we can learn gradually to inhale and exhale in a manner that is inexpressibly wonderful because it is divine. For then we shall constantly be breathing with the very "breath" of God. . . . Let us take courage then, and sing with the Psalmist: "I opened my mouth and gasped for breath because I longed for thy commandments." . . . It is by prayer that we lay open our souls to God and seek to "breathe" His life. The supreme object of prayer is the fulfilment of God's Will.[10]

Now create a prayer that you are able to say in the span of just one single breath. Write down your ideas.

# FUEL UP

## HILDEGARD VON BINGEN (1098-1179)

*Feeling sad and oh so blue?* Hildegard von Bingen believed you could eat your way out of melancholy—with a healing helping of her cookies of joy: crunchy treats that delivered the power of hearty spelt flour combined with warming spices, guaranteed to "calm all bitterness of the heart and mind, open your heart and impaired senses, and make your mind cheerful."[1]

Cookies of joy—which also went by the name nerve cookies—brought balance back to a body afflicted by an overabundance of black bile, which Hildegard reckoned to be the source of evil and depression. Her first weapon against this darkness was spelt, an ancient, unmodified version of wheat, which she extolled as a "rich and powerful" cereal grain best served hot to "create a happy mind and put joy in the human disposition."[2] Next, she mixed in generous doses of nutmeg, cinnamon, and clove—warming stimulants believed to energize the heart, brain, and sensations and to establish an overall positive attitude.[3]

Hildegard von Bingen was neither a baker nor a chef, not exactly. She was a renowned, visionary abbess, a spiritual teacher who firmly believed that vigorous bodies, clear minds, and trusting spirits require excellent nutrition. Her theories on food were no side hobby but central to her God-centered view of reality. *Physica*, Hildegard's twelfth-century book on health and healing, begins with an account of the world's creation in which "all of the elements served humankind, and sensing that humans were alive, they busied themselves in aiding the humans' life in every way" by providing "vital energy" through beneficial herbs, fruits, certain animals and fish, and plants that "are gentle on the digestion and possess a happy nature, producing happiness in anyone who eats them."[4] In Hildegard's theology, the natural world is abundant with blessed sustenance, remedies, and delights, all eager to be tasted.

To this day, the nuns at St. Hildegard Abbey, founded along Germany's Rhine River in 1165, still carry on their founder's culinary traditions, making and selling cookies of joy along with galangal-ginger treats, wine, and a selection of herbal liqueurs and teas harvested from the abbey's garden and vineyard. A plaque in the gift shop celebrates the work of the faithful sisters' hands: "Humanity, take a good look at yourself. Inside you've got heaven and earth, all of creation. You're a world—everything is hidden in you."[5]

In the chapel, the sisters sing a harmonious chant composed by Hildegard in praise of God, the living Light, who says, "I am the breeze that nurtures all things green. I encourage blossoms to flourish with ripening fruits. I adorn all the earth. I am the rain coming from the dew that causes the grass to laugh with the joy of life."[6] The medieval abbess calls us all to cultivate and cocreate, that we may savor the flavors of the earthly which are good gifts of the heavenly.

# GOODBYE, TWINKIES

The bell rang: lunchtime at last. I pulled the crushed brown paper bag out of my cubby and lined up with the other third graders. At the cafeteria table, I spread out my lunch: beef stew, a pear, three prunes, a sliced green pepper. Ugh. My parents were out of town on a mission trip, and my grandmother had taken complete charge of us five kids. Until my mom got back, there would be no Cheetos for me. No grape jelly and Jif peanut butter on Wonder Bread. No chocolate milk. And worst of all? No Twinkies.

Ah, Twinkies, beloved snack food of my childhood: made up of three dozen multisyllabic ingredients combined to form a cylindrical sponge cake injected with three gobs of white vanilla-like fluff. Packaged in airtight plastic, Twinkies are the stuff of legend, still edible, so they say, after decades on the shelf. My grandmother, Betty Weible Sweet, would have none of such foolishness. She'd majored in domestic science at Kansas State University in the 1920s and knew a thing or two about nutrition.

She tossed out the Lucky Charms cereal and served us steaming oatmeal loaded with raisins. She sat us down to dinners of spinach, sweet potatoes, and roasted chicken (yay!) or liver with onions (gasp!). Dessert was homemade applesauce or stewed rhubarb, products of my grandfather's three-acre garden. No day was complete without a generous sprinkling of Kretschmer wheat germ. We children hid our lima beans in our napkins and counted the days till Mom would return and bring back edible meals of Hamburger Helper, fried Spam, and her signature macaroni and cheese.

Given the chance, Betty Sweet and Hildegard von Bingen would likely have talked for hours, trading recipes and opinions about the wellness that begins on the inside. I can imagine Hildegard nodding her head as Betty says, "Fennel tea is the very best thing for a headache."[7] And the insistence on a hot breakfast? Totally on the same page there. Betty and Hildegard were way ahead of their time with the whole-grains hype. Scientists have even tested Hildegard's claim, "Spelt is the very best grain. It provides for good flesh and good blood,"[8] and found that this medieval form of wheat is easy to digest and stimulates the immune system with rich micronutrients, vitamins, prebiotics, and anti-inflammatory and antidepressant properties.

These days I've been reading *This Is Your Brain on Food* by Harvard's Uma Naidoo, a pioneer in the emerging field of nutritional psychiatry. She has me thinking about the Gut-Brain Axis, which facilitates connections between what I eat, how I feel, and even how I behave, powered by the bacteria that live in my gut. My brain, that most complex, energy-consuming organ in my body, is always "on," choreographing my thoughts, movements, breathing, heartbeats, senses, and moods, sustaining me even while I'm asleep.[9]

I don't need Naidoo to tell me that my brain runs best on premium fuel. (I guess Twinkies are out.) I'm sure my grandmother would take it one step further, insisting that since God created my body to function on healthy food, then eating right is a kind of spiritual care. She might even quote Hildegard von Bingen: "When the body and soul work in perfect harmony, they receive the supreme reward of joy and health."[10] Who could argue with that?

## TRY THIS

Hungry yet? Skim these Hildegard-inspired recipes and tips.

### Start Small

There is a well-known Chinese proverb that proclaims "A journey of a thousand miles begins with a single step." I take that to mean, "No need to swear off *all* junk food just yet." Start with something you can reasonably do in the next twenty-four hours. The American Heart Association recommends two servings of fruit and two and a half servings of vegetables.[11] Could all that fit into one salad or smoothie, I wonder?

**Get Going**

Choose a cookbook or go online, select three recipes that you find super simple, quick, and appealing, and write up your grocery list. Or just improvise with my no-cook, no-rules recipe. Seriously, a first grader could prepare this.

## FEEL-GOOD OVERNIGHT OATS

Find a mason jar or glass container and pour in

- 1 part uncooked old-fashioned oats (or cooked spelt if you're daring)
- ⅛ part chia seeds (if you have them)
- 1½ parts dairy or plant-based milk

Stir gently. From here, add what you like and what you have on hand, such as

- maple syrup, honey, or jam
- Greek or vegan yogurt
- a splash of vanilla extract
- chopped nuts
- fresh or dried fruit
- coconut
- chocolate chips

Cover the container and stash it in the fridge overnight. Make a batch of jars to last you several days. You can eat the mixture cold, right from the jar. Or heat it up to make Hildegard and Betty happy.

## Put the Kettle On

For thousands of years, people all over the world have been drinking tea for its health benefits. At the very least, tea helps us relax, which is no small thing. Hildegard is partial to lavender tea: "Whoever cooks lavender in wine, or if she has no wine, in honey and water, and frequently drinks it when it is warm, will lessen the pain in her liver and lungs, and the stuffiness in her chest. It also makes her thinking and disposition pure."[12]

Hildegard loved warming spices too. Studies show that turmeric's antioxidant properties boost the immune system and brain.[13]

## TURMERIC TEA

Combine the following in a small pot and simmer on low for 10 minutes:

- ½ teaspoon ground turmeric
- ¼ teaspoon black pepper
- 2 tablespoons lemon juice
- 2 cups water

Add a teaspoon or two of honey.

## Eat for Healing

Believe it or not, Dr. Naidoo, the nutritional psychiatrist, recommends the following recipe, with ingredients containing tryptophan, omega-3s, and vitamins, for her patients experiencing anxiety.[14]

## AVOCADO HUMMUS

Combine in a food processor:

- 1 large ripe avocado, skin and pit removed
- 2 cups chickpeas
- ⅓ cup tahini paste
- ¼ cup fresh lime juice
- 1 clove garlic

- 1 teaspoon kosher salt
- ¼ teaspoon black pepper
- ½ teaspoon cumin
- ¼ teaspoon paprika
- ½ cup cilantro
- 2 tablespoons olive oil

Put the hummus in a bowl, drizzle with olive oil, and top with

- 1 tablespoon sliced, toasted almonds
- ¼ cup chopped parsley

Serve with whole-grain toast or fresh vegetables.

And we can't leave out Hildegard von Bingen's cookie recipe. The nuns of St. Hildegard's Abbey are pleased to share their secrets.

## HILDEGARD VON BINGEN'S COOKIES OF JOY (OR NERVE COOKIES)

- 12 tablespoons butter
- ¾ cup brown sugar
- ⅓ cup raw honey
- 4 egg yolks
- 2½ cups spelt flour (you can usually find it in the baking aisle)
- 1 teaspoon salt
- 1 tablespoon nutmeg
- 1 tablespoon cinnamon
- 1 teaspoon cloves

Preheat the oven to 375 degrees.

Melt the butter, then add it to a medium bowl with the sugar, honey, and egg yolks. Beat gently, then fold in the rest of the ingredients. Refrigerate the dough for an hour.

Flour a surface and then roll out the cookie dough until about a ¼-inch thick. Cut the dough into circles using a cookie cutter or drinking glass and place on a baking sheet lined with parchment paper. Bake for 10 minutes or until golden brown.

# KEEP ON WALKING

## MARGERY KEMPE (ca. 1373–ca. 1438)

*What possessed Margery Kempe* to set out from England for Jerusalem, Rome, Assisi, Santiago de Compostela, and beyond? She had a comfortable life in England. As the mayor's daughter and a businesswoman who'd run the largest brewery in Lynn, Margery was the wife of a good man and mother to fourteen children. A respectable, pious matron. Why would she up and go halfway across the known world, alone?

By Margery's account, it all started with a powerful calling. "I was prompted in my soul," she explains, "to visit certain places for my spiritual good." She was possessed by the desire to walk, quite literally, in the steps of Jesus. "I had a great longing to see for myself the place where he was born," to see and touch the ground where Jesus lived, suffered, and died.[1]

She would also travel to Spain to approach the place where the bones of St. James are enshrined in Santiago de Compostela. Rome, Assisi, and shrines in Canterbury, Norway, and Germany were sacred places holding holy power that one could experience only in person. No domestic duty or familial responsibility—the obligations of her womanly state—could hold Margery Kempe back from her personal, spiritual quest.

A medieval pilgrimage was no luxury tour (though months of travel and thousands of miles required serious money). Before they set out, pilgrims of the day wrote their last wills, fully expecting that they might die along the way, victims of disease, robbers, drownings at sea, accidents on land, even starvation or enslavement. It took Margery Kempe, short on funds, two years to even get out of her hometown. At last, God prompted her to get going, saying, "Set out on your way, daughter, in the name of Jesus. . . . I shall help you with your every need. I shall go with you and support you in every place you come to."[2]

Even as Lynn's townspeople mocked Margery for her noisy religious fervor and her children clamored for her attention, the voice of Jesus nudged her on. She was sure she heard Jesus say, *"Never fear. I will love you always. I go with you. I am at your side. Do not be anxious, for I am a hidden God within you."*[3]

Hers was a Jesus who called her to walk not only to her local church or into her closet for prayer but also out into the wild world. "Where God is, there is heaven also: God is in your soul with many an angel guarding you night and day," he promised Margery. "I go with you. Even when you leave town, remember that I journey with you, helping and keeping you with every step."[4]

And so Margery Kempe settled her affairs, received her husband's permission, said farewell, and set out. In the span of three years, she would make it to Jerusalem, Rome, Assisi, and Santiago de Compostela, driven by an unflagging, all-consuming devotion to the suffering Jesus who accompanied her, saying, "Talk to me with your innermost heart."[5]

Often overcome by worship, she was known to weep and wail so loudly that one preacher banned her from church as an intolerable disruption. Her relentless obsession with God got on the nerves of her fellow travelers, who refused to eat with her, cheated her, and organized travel plans behind her back. Margery considered it all persecution, proof of her spiritual sacrifice and her commitment to encounter God with her very body. Trekking across the icy Alps, begging in Rome, stuck for weeks waiting for a ship, trudging the remote trails of Spain, she would journey on ever more deeply into the physical places and presence of God.

At age sixty, Margery Kempe, who could neither read nor write, managed to find scribes to write down her story, the first autobiography in the English language. This account of her pilgrimage to Canterbury is typical: "I was overjoyed in our Lord, who always sent me help and support at times such as these." She goes on, "So I thanked him with many devout tears and much sobbing and weeping, for it was the same in every place I had been to, so many times that it was impossible to tell, on this side of the sea or on the other, always the same whether on water or dry land. Blessed may God be."[6]

## FOLLOW THE YELLOW ARROWS

The sunlight filters through the chestnut trees in this forest in northern Spain, illuminating a divide in the path ahead. With no GPS map to help, we stand and wonder whether to go up through the eucalyptus grove or down the rocky slope. Then Nan spots it: a yellow arrow hand-painted on a rock, pointing right. Here is the way, the way to Santiago. So uphill we go.

Each year, thousands of people walk the medieval pilgrimage routes along the Way of St. James; whether they set out from the French Pyrenees mountains, the Portuguese coast, or somewhere in between, all paths lead to the cathedral in Santiago de Compostela. For eight days, my daughter and I have been walking the Camino de Santiago westward through Galicia, following yellow arrows and scallop shell signs: waymarks set in stone and concrete, painted on walls, lampposts, streets, and stone walls. Plaques count down the kilometers that remain to the cathedral.

Along the route, Nan and I pass by some pilgrims, and others pass us. We strangers greet one another with "Buen Camino!"

and often fall in step for an hour or end up chatting outside a village café, easy companions headed in the same direction, all marked by sturdy footwear, backpacks, water bottles, and trekking poles, carrying the scallop shells that identify us as pilgrims.

Every morning we set out to move our bodies uphill and down, stumbling or grumbling at times, stopping to catch our breath, taking in a golden vista, sheltering from a rain shower. "This is not a competition!" we murmur as a runner sweeps by on the trail. All the while, our buzzing brains let go, little by little, lulled by the simple rhythm of the walk. Far from the push of daily tasks, we follow the yellow arrows wherever they lead. For these blessed days, there is nothing we must do but keep to the Camino.

Early in this journey, I'd fretted about many things. Would my temperamental knee flare up, sidelining me with pain? Would our Band-Aids and moleskin patches ward off blisters? What about tomorrow's weather app forecast: 90 percent chance of rain and high winds? Were the passports and credit card securely stowed in my pocket? Was the insulin cold enough? An early signpost as we left the mountain village of O'Cebreiro unnerved me: 158 kilometers to Santiago! Would it be too hot, too hard, too much? Yet today I find that my body feels better after walking fourteen miles than it does at home when I get up at the end of nine hours at my desk. We are, truly, designed to move, walk, scramble, and sweat.

"Why are *you* walking the Camino?" some ask. Margaret Kempe, who went this way six hundred years ago, would likely have answered without hesitation: "I heard the voice of Jesus loud and clear, beckoning me to Santiago, so that's where I'm headed." Many pilgrims still walk with spiritual intentions—to encounter God, to seek healing, to savor the Spirit's presence, to experience grace in a physical, sacred space, to join the cloud of believers who have traced these paths.

Others take to the Camino not out of prayerful devotion but to work through a personal loss, discern new purpose, meet the challenge of a rigorous trek. Clusters of friends chatter in the sunshine, while others walk in solitude. Nan and I meet Pablo, a burned-out corporate exec on his first break in three years; Viktor, newly retired from teaching; Katrin, learning to navigate the constraints of a medical condition.

Why do I walk the Camino? Imagining this trip, I'd wondered if Margery's Jesus might speak a transforming word to me, offer a flash of vivid insight. But now, here on the Way, I'm simply grateful to walk peaceably beside my daughter, a young woman who is inexpressibly dear to me. She goes ahead by a few steps, setting the pace, mile upon mile. Over these days, we talk about everything and about nothing, marvel at the lyre-shaped horns of the sleek, brown cattle. We lure cats out of haystacks, pick up glossy chestnuts along the trail, stretch out on benches, pull our trail shoes off with a sigh, rub our feet. We listen to the quiet.

Yes, there will be celebratory photos when we reach our destination; we will brandish our Compostela certificates awarded by the church's Pilgrim's Reception Office, dance to the welcoming bagpipe, and attend the pilgrims' mass in the cathedral. But the deepest grace of all is just here: in the walking.

# TRY THIS

People take to walking for all kinds of reasons. What are yours?

### Walk to Think

Perhaps it's a coincidence, but history is filled with brilliant thinkers who were also obsessive walkers, people who set out day or night to solve problems, shake loose ideas, and spark creativity.

There is something about walking that enlivens and stimulates our thoughts, an experience confirmed by researchers. For many of us, when we stay in one place, we can hardly think at all; our bodies have to be on the move to set our minds going.[7] Are you ready to experience the power of walking?

- Take a moment to identify one problem or situation that's troubling your mind today.
  Describe it here:

  _____

  _____

  _____

- Now head outside or hop on a treadmill and walk, dedicating your walk to mindful consideration of your problem, pushing yourself to think freely and without judgment, generating as many options, answers, or ideas as you are able.
- As your time concludes, consider this: Did the experience of walking shift anything in your thinking?

## Walk to Hope

What inner or outer journey might you be feeling called to begin—in the coming days, months, or year? As you read God's call to Margery Kempe, listen for God's word to you.

> Set out on your way, daughter, in the name of Jesus, for I am
>     truly the spirit of God;
> I shall help you with your every need.
> I shall go with you and support you in every place you come
>     to. . . .
> Do not be anxious for truly I am a hidden God within you.
> I journey with you.[8]

What feelings, images, or ideas come up for you? Draw or write about them here.

## Walk to Pray

Margery Kempe may have possessed a small prayer book to accompany her private devotions, a volume like the *Belles Heures of Jean de Berry*, a beautifully illuminated manuscript from 1409. It contains a prayer to accompany you on your next walk, whether it be a stroll around the block or a pilgrimage of many miles.

> O God, who granted to the [children] of Israel to pass
>     through the middle of the sea with dry steps,
> and who revealed thee to the three wise men through the
>     guidance of a star,
> grant us, we beg thee, a prosperous path and calm weather,
> so that we might be worthy of arriving at the place where
>     we are going and, finally,
> at the gate of eternal happiness.[9]

Or you may prefer the simplicity of this Celtic walking prayer:

> I on your path, O God.
> You, O God, on my way.

*Jesus Christ is not only with us in lonely hours;*
*Jesus Christ, God himself, speaks to us from every human being;*
*the other person, this enigmatic, impenetrable You,*
*is God's claim on us;*
*indeed, the holy God is in each person we encounter.*

—Dietrich Bonhoeffer (1906–1945),
The Collected Sermons of Dietrich Bonhoeffer

In pursuit of an answer to the ancient human question "Who am I?" I have been practicing bringing my inner attention to the moments of my extraordinary, ordinary life. As I do, another question emerges: "*Whose* am I?" Eyes open now, my vision draws me outward, to my inextricable bonds with other humans, creatures, and the earth itself—a vast, complex community of relationships.

I am one small, fragile being among innumerable fragile beings. What now?

"Only connect!" people often say, though they haven't often explained how. In search of what this might mean, I turn to six more wise guides. They call me, first of all, toward gratitude for the interdependent web created intentionally by God, divinely crafted for our mutual flourishing. Through art and song, they observe, investigate, and portray the exquisite world and its varied inhabitants. They speak up and act out on behalf of all who are at risk, from our human neighbors to our planet home and its imperiled climate, oxygen, plants, creatures, and water.

These spiritual teachers dare to ask God challenging questions, in search of even deeper understandings of who we are and how to live. They urge me to pray for God's wisdom. They invite me to seek my own particular path of service in this world, confident that the path of true connection is the certain way to joy.

So reach out. Dare to connect.

# PLANT A TREE

## WANGARI MAATHAI (1940–2011)

*When little Wangari went out to collect firewood* near her home in the Kenyan highlands, she was careful to heed her mother's warning: "Don't ever break any branches off the fig tree!" Mindful that the fig was "a tree of God" to be protected from harm, she lingered in the sparkling green shade of its branches and played in the clear water of the spring bubbling up by its roots. This quiet hideaway was the source of a great river.[1] Years later, Wangari would recall the village women's reverence for flourishing figs, their spiritual and cultural commitment to the trees that held the rich soil together, reduced erosion and landslides, and preserved the fresh streams that nourished a biodiversity of plant and animal life.

As a postdoctoral scientist conducting research outside Nairobi, Wangari returned to her family's old village and was grieved by what she found. The ancient indigenous forest had been replaced by commercial tea and coffee agricultural tracts; the sacred fig tree of her childhood had been cut down to make space for cash crops. All had changed under British colonialists, who viewed trees as timber, elephants as commercial stock, and cheetahs as skins for sale. "As we were to learn," Wangari mused, "if you can sell it, you can forget about protecting it."[2] With the sacrifice of the shading tree, the flowing stream had long dried up, leaving only a patch of bare ground where nothing grew—on the very land that had abundantly fed untold generations of Wangari's ancestors.[3]

Dr. Maathai questioned rural women like her sisters and aunts, women now suffering from poverty, malnutrition, and a lack of clean water, firewood, and fodder for livestock. "As I sat listening to the women talk about water, energy, and nutrition, I could see that everything that they lacked depended on the environment," she recalled, "and I have always been interested in finding solutions."[4]

This woman set out not to start a revolution but to solve a problem. "It just came to me," she said simply. "Why not plant trees?" And so Wangari Maathai's Green Belt Movement began, an effort that has recruited hundreds of thousands of women to plant more than forty *million* trees in Kenya alone.[5]

As long as Wangari and her women busied themselves with only growing and watering seedlings, they were left in peace. But as the Green Belt Movement developed, it planted more than trees; it planted ideas about managing natural resources efficiently, sustainably, and equitably. It planted ideas about democracy and human rights.

Wangari became convinced that to heal their communities and their nation, the Kenyan people needed to identify the deeper roots of their disempowerment, face up to the culpability of their government, and acknowledge their personal and communal responsibilities. As a person of Christian faith, Wangari remembered the disciples' words to a suffering beggar: "In the name of Jesus Christ of Nazareth, rise up and walk!"[6] This would be her lifelong motto.

"Why are we robbing ourselves of a future?" she challenged those attending her civic and environmental education seminars.[7] In pursuit of the answer, Wangari Maathai and her Green Belt women would face intense trials: harassment, slander, imprisonment, and violence.

Though Kenya gained independence in 1963, by the late 1980s a repressive regime was in power. This regime opposed

Wangari's campaign to save Uhuru Park, Nairobi's last surviving green urban refuge, from destruction. By raising a public alarm throughout Kenya and around the world, Wangari stopped a sixty-story tower from being built, but not before the corrupt government and its allies had waged a war of obstruction against her and the "clique of women" who violated "the African tradition" of respecting men and staying quiet. The Green Belt Movement persisted until the Uhuru Park project was abandoned at last; then Wangari announced, "Let's go to the park and dance, a dance of victory!"[8] And dance they did.

The struggles for environmental protections were far from over. When Green Belt was wrongly evicted from its offices, Wangari moved the staff into her tiny home. She lost her university teaching job and was blocked from running for public office, beaten, placed under house arrest. Yet she defended the Karura Forest, opposed illegal land grabs, exposed governmental and corporate malfeasance, and participated in hunger strikes on behalf of Kenyans brutally silenced for prodemocratic activities. And she kept on planting trees.

One morning in 2004, Wangari Maathai received an unexpected phone call from Oslo: she had been awarded the Nobel Peace Prize. Over the clamor of journalists, she did what was second nature: she called for a tree seedling and a shovel. Describing that moment as she faced Mt. Kenya in the distance, she said, "I kneeled down, put my hands in the red soil, warm from the sun, settled the tree seedling in the ground. They handed me a bucket of clean water and I watered the tree. . . . At that moment I felt I stood on sacred ground."[9]

# TEN TREES

It's a perfect August morning, this anniversary of my father's death. Sitting in the backyard with my coffee and laptop, I'm shaded by the emerald leaves of the great oak overhead. High up in its branches, a pair of red-tailed hawks have made a nest. An avid gardener once lived here and planted the glossy magnolias, the looming pines, the leggy azaleas, trees that flourish in Virginia. How different things are far away in Kenya, where a fourth consecutive year of drought has yielded unabated misery.

On my computer, I'm watching a documentary about Wangari Maathai, the woman known as Mama Miti, Mother of Trees. She addresses Trinity United Church of Christ: "I want to urge you that as we leave church today you look at the trees and the bushes with a special respect, and you thank them for taking care of the carbon dioxide you breathe out." She tells the congregation, "The actual process of planting a tree is very spiritual. You're almost repeating the acts of God. There is something about touching the soil and going down on your knees. It's almost like you are humbling yourself to the wonders of creation."[10]

A natural-born preacher, Wangari Maathai urges us to turn appreciation for the natural world into action: "We each need at least ten trees to take care of our own carbon dioxide, and so if you don't have ten trees somewhere where you can say 'These are my trees,' then you are using somebody else's trees, and you ought to get up and plant your own."[11]

I have to admit that I am most definitely using somebody else's trees—nine, to be specific. The only tree that I can rightly call "my tree" is a crape myrtle some friends gave to me. After my father died three summers ago, there it was by my front door, a twiggy seedling in a three-gallon container, a note tied to one branch: "We are so sorry for your loss." The next time a guy with a lawn mower paid a visit, I asked him to plant it in a sunny corner of the garden, where it has been growing ever since.

Now nearly four feet tall, the crape myrtle carries on bravely, despite my failure to fertilize or water it. This morning, thinking of my dad, I happen to notice that the tree has sent out a few deep-pink blossoms, lovely crinkled flowers with a crepe-like texture. In the oak's shade, I turn to Wangari Maathai's autobiography, *Unbowed*, the part where she writes, "Trees have been an essential part of my life and provided me with many lessons. Trees are living symbols of peace and hope."[12]

A tree has its roots in the soil and yet reaches the sky, a living reminder that "in order to aspire we need to be grounded, and no matter how high we go it is from our roots that we draw sustenance."[13] To all of us who have had success, she says, we cannot forget where we came from. I'm humbled for the moment by Wangari's words, by the memory of a father who loved the woods and who loved me, by the conviction that I rarely appreciate these trees in my own yard.

In her last years, Wangari Maathai embarked on an ambitious new project: the planting of a billion trees worldwide. She called on Christians like me to set aside Easter Monday as a day to plant trees. Consider that Christ was crucified on the cross, she would say. Somebody had to go into the forest, cut a tree, and chop it up for Jesus to be crucified. What an appropriate gesture it would be to plant trees as a great celebration of Christ's resurrection, in thanksgiving for our own regeneration, revival, of being reborn, of finding salvation.

I open my phone and mark my calendar with a reminder, a small note that will pop up on Ash Wednesday of next year. What better way to spend the Lenten season than to plan for the Easter Monday to come, to restore the earth in some small way? In the late summer sun, I promise Mama Miti that I will plant nine seedlings next spring—trees that I will be able to call my own.

# TRY THIS

How does Wangari Maathai's story resonate with your own story? Consider that question through one of these prompts.

## Formed by Faith?

> *The trees of the field will yield their fruit and the ground will yield its crops; the people will be secure in the land. They will know that I am the LORD, when I break the bars of their yoke and rescue them from the hands of those who enslaved them.*
>
> —*Ezekiel 34:27, opening epigraph in*
> *Wangari Maathai,* Unbowed

While Wangari Maathai was deeply influenced by her Catholic faith and the nuns who educated her as a college biology major, she never lost the reverent care that her Kikuyu ancestors held for the natural world.

Reflect on your own upbringing:

- What did the community of your childhood teach about the environment?
- What does the verse from Ezekiel say about trees, people, and God?
- Does your personal spirituality connect with your ideas around creation care? What does that look like in the practices of your daily life?

## Be Like the Hummingbird

Wangari Maathai ends her memoir with a Japanese folktale. The story goes that one day a massive fire broke out in the forest. All the animals, as the flames came ever closer, decided to save themselves. As they watched in dismay from the edge of the forest, feeling overwhelmed and helpless as the flames engulfed their homes, they saw the hummingbird flying above them. "I'm going to do something about the fire!" she cried as she flew to a nearby stream, scooped up a drop of water in her beak, and dropped it onto the fire.

Back and forth she flew, from stream to inferno, focused and tireless, without losing speed or patience. Each time she carried a droplet and let it fall on the flames. The other animals looked on in disbelief. "You are too small!" they shouted. "What do you think you're doing? You cannot hope to put out the fire!" As she dove again, the hummingbird turned to the animals and exclaimed, "I'm doing the best I can!" This is what we are called to do, no matter who or where we are, or what our capabilities. We are called to do the best we can![14]

- If you were to place yourself in this story, which character would you be? What would you say and do?
- When you consider the current state of the earth, what thoughts and feelings come to mind?
- What is one hummingbird-sized action you might take to protect our natural home?

### Plant Your Ten Trees

Even if you don't want to get your hands dirty planting seedlings, you can support a nonprofit that offers tree planting sponsorships. Through its Plant a Billion Trees forest restoration campaign, the Nature Conservancy is working to plant a billion trees around the planet to slow the connected crises of climate change and biodiversity loss. For each $20 donation to their Gift a Tree program, the Nature Conservancy will plant and maintain ten seedling trees in critical forests around the globe.[15]

# SAY THANK YOU

## CAEDMON (ca. 657–684)

*Caedmon dreaded the moment that was sure to arrive.* The remnants of the grand feast had been cleared away and the harp had come out; the evening's merry entertainment began by the light of the blazing logs in the abbey's great hall. In medieval tradition, the harp was passed from one dinner guest to the next, each singing in turn to please the crowd with improvised ballads of adventure, romance, and battle.

Shy, awkward Caedmon, knowing that his turn with the harp was at hand, watched for his chance to slip from the table, to escape into the shadows and away—back to the cowshed, where the warm breath of the cattle soothed the shame of his illiteracy, his inarticulate words, his cracking voice, the many faults that brought laughter and derision from the clever, educated monks. Poor Caedmon, the least of the lay brothers, believed he was worthy only to lodge with the animals.

The ancient story goes that, deeply asleep that night, Caedmon dreamed a vivid dream. He heard a voice saying, "Caedmon, sing something to Me." Even in his sleep, Caedmon stuttered his excuse: he could not sing, he knew no poems, it was no use. But the voice commanded again, "Sing!" "What shall I sing?" Caedmon asked, delaying the inevitable embarrassment. "Sing the beginning of created things!" Then in the darkness of his dream, Caedmon opened his mouth and, astonished, heard his own voice singing, "Now we must praise the Protector of the heavenly kingdom!" Another line followed: "The power of the Creator and His wise design, the deeds of the Father of glory." On and on Caedmon went, spinning a new hymn of gratitude to the Maker and Sustainer of all reality. "For each of His wonders, the eternal Lord established a beginning."[1]

Upon waking at dawn, Caedmon remembered it all. He could even sing again this miraculous canticle of thanks and praise to God that he had composed in his sleep. Caedmon recounted his dream to his boss, the steward, who rushed to the abbess with the tale. Abbess Hilda tested the clumsy, unschooled herdsman and found that what he said was true: in the night he had been transformed into a poet of sacred mysteries, a singer of hymns that overflowed with thankfulness. Hilda took Caedmon out of the barn and into the community, where he was made a monk. The other brothers taught him all the biblical stories, from the creation of the world to its redemption in Christ. Whatever he learned Caedmon reproduced in such beautiful and touching verse that "his teachers were glad to become his hearers."[2] The lonely cowherd who'd had only livestock for company now lived as a beloved and accomplished member of the abbey. To the end of his life, Caedmon—known today as the first Old English poet—created unexcelled poems, ever grateful to the beckoning God who stirs in the night.

# INSUPPRESSIBLE GRATITUDE

I was surprised to find myself crying as I listened to the news report: Dallas Willard had died at the age of seventy-eight. Over the years, I'd been influenced by this American philosopher and teacher of spiritual formation—but it wasn't sorrow I was feeling. My tears were the wondrous kind, the kind you mean when you say "I was moved to tears," and were provoked by a small detail in the story of Willard's death. After a year suffering with pancreatic cancer, hospitalized and in tremendous pain, Dallas Willard had leaned his head slightly back, closed his eyes, and said, in a clear voice, "Thank you."[3] His last words. The friend at his bedside was certain that Dallas was speaking to another Presence in the room—a vividly real and now finally visible-to-him God. Imagining the scene, I asked myself, "Will a simple thank you be in my mouth as I take my final breath? Dare I hope to go with gratitude when my earthly life ends?"

Dallas Willard's story was fraught with hardship. Born into rural, Depression-era Missouri, troubled by grief, poverty, anxiety, and self-doubt, he found God when he was at the end of his rope. He grew into a compassionate, wise guide not by happy accident but by sustained intention. In the company of a present and personal God, Dallas not only taught about Christian spiritual disciplines but also put them into practice. Over time, he was transformed into a spiritually alive person, radiant in life and radiant in death.

"How can I be more grateful too?" I would ask Dallas. I find that he has already replied, writing, "Holy delight is the great antidote to despair and is a wellspring of genuine gratitude."[4] Dwelling on the greatness and goodness of God and seeing my life and the world as God's work and as God's gift to me—this is where thankfulness begins. The act of saying thank you disciplines me to see the light and to hear a different voice, shifting me away from negativity and toward hope.

I want to become more like Dallas, who himself came to inhabit a godlike well-being in God's companionship and kingdom. He knew what it was to be counted among those commonly thought to be ruined—the poor, the depressed, the persecuted— yet he nourished, even there, an "insuppressible" gratitude for the life without lack that Jesus came to give. Dallas's habit of celebration expressed a faith that "sometimes becomes a delirious joy coursing through our bodily being, when we really begin to see how great and lovely God is and how good he has been to us."[5]

I am a fearful human and, fragile as I am, lean toward negativity. Yet life owes me nothing. All good things are a gift. Though I tend to live in my own head, Caedmon and Dallas gave thanks with their *whole* selves: body, mind, and spirit. They viewed life with curiosity and attention. Through their eyes, I glimpse the bigger view of God's grandeur and grace, and something alters inside. How can I help but praise the holy Guardian, the One who made heaven to be a roof and earth to be a wondrous home for all of us?

I even feel the pull to dance with the community of the created: the miraculous, living earth and the generations of grateful people who have come before. I resolve to practice the ancient morning prayer of Judaism: "I thank you, living and enduring King, for you have graciously returned my soul within me. Great is your faithfulness." Or to simply say, "Thank you."

# TRY THIS

Practice one or two invitations into thankfulness. The others will be here for you to try out later.

### Gratitude Warm-up

There is a saying attributed to G. K. Chesterton that "gratitude is happiness doubled by wonder." Take some time to reflect—through the fresh eyes of *wonder*—on all that brings *happiness* into your life. Begin by completing these prompts:

One person who makes my life richer is . . .
An ability or skill of mine that I feel fortunate to have is . . .
Something I've loved about this day so far is . . .
One part of my everyday routine that I savor is . . .
A wonderful thing about my neighborhood or community is . . .
One incredibly beautiful landscape I've seen is . . .

Can you take the next step and give thanks? Take time to pray or meditate in the spirit of gratitude.

## O Taste and See

Close your eyes and take in a few deep, relaxing breaths. Bring your awareness to your five physical senses, one by one. Taste. See. Touch. Smell. Hear. Let your mind wander back to one rich, rewarding memory connected with each sensation and craft a prayer to the One who surrounds you with good things.

O God who created this body of mine,
I am thankful that I can taste . . .
I am thankful that I can see . . .
I am thankful that I can touch . . .
I am thankful that I can smell . . .
I am thankful that I can hear . . .

## When You See Something, Say Something

As you go through this day, actively look for strangers who are taking small, constructive actions—and then speak words of grateful acknowledgment to them.

- Is someone cleaning an office or airport bathroom? Recognize their effort.
- Is someone taking your payment in a store? Say a kind word.
- Is someone pulling weeds in a park or cleaning the street? Call out the difference they make.

Keep your thank-you simple and sincere. Make eye contact. You'll both feel good.

### Get Philosophical

Psychologist Robert Emmons maintains that a posture of gratitude is the truest approach to life.[6] Consider this: you and I did not fashion ourselves. We certainly did not birth ourselves. From the beginning to the end of our lives, each and every one of us is profoundly dependent on other people and on their help, gifts, and kindness—and on nature's largesse too. Given that life is about giving, receiving, and repaying, thankfulness is a right and essential quality of flourishing.

Can you think of one personal story that supports the claim that gratitude is the truest approach to life?

### Better Late Than Never

Collect a few notecards, envelopes, and stamps. Take a few minutes to think about the past. Go back as far as you like. Now write a note of thanks to someone in your life who has never been properly thanked for their kindness, whether large or small. Address the envelope and put it in the mailbox. Better yet, deliver and read your letter in person. Emails and phone calls count too.

## Move Your Thanks

> *Blessed be G*OD—
> *he heard me praying.*
> *He proved he's on my side;*
> *I've thrown my lot in with him.*
> *Now I'm jumping for joy,*
> *and shouting and singing my thanks to him!*

—Psalm 28:6–7 The Message

This exclamation from the psalmist calls for movement, doesn't it? Take that energy and walk, jump, shout, or sing out your thanksgiving. Feel the joy of praising the God from whom all blessings flow!

# PRAY YOUR ANYTHING

## AMANDA BERRY SMITH (1837–1915)

*On the face of it,* Amanda Berry Smith had little reason to celebrate. She'd been born into slavery in Maryland; even in freedom, her labors as a laundress left her starved and impoverished. Amanda suffered the grief of abandonment by two husbands, the deaths of four of her five children, and the pressure of iron-hard racism at every turn. Yet this same woman, who couldn't pay the five dollars for her son's funeral, wrote, "I was wild with delight and joy; it seemed to me as if I would split!" To her, even a well-worn ironing board glowed with a halo of light as she smacked it, shouting, "Glory to God, I have got religion!"[1]

She hadn't always felt this delight. In her autobiography, Amanda writes about her intense, prolonged struggle to encounter God. One morning, overcome by doubt and sorrow, she voiced her frustrations. "I seemed to get to the end of everything," she would later recall. "I did not know what else to say or do." In her desperation, she cried, "O, Lord, if Thou wilt help me, I will believe in Thee."[2]

In the very act of prayer, Amanda felt peace and joy flood her body. She sprang to her feet, so stunned by the blazing light within and around her that she dashed to the dining room, expecting to find a different woman looking back at her from the mirror on the wall. Though her familiar physical self—and the grim challenges of her circumstances—remained unchanged,

Amanda would forever remember the moment when God made her new all over and divinity re-enchanted her world.

As described in Amanda Berry Smith's autobiography, her days are saturated in prayer: from morning till night she converses with God, and she argues with the devil too. She recounts days occupied with work while she is simultaneously thinking and talking to God. "It is not necessary to be a nun or be isolated away off in some deep retirement," she tells her readers, for "though your hands are employed in doing your daily business, it is no bar to the soul's communion with Jesus. Many times over my wash-tub and ironing table, and while making my bed and sweeping my house and washing my dishes I have had some of the richest blessings."[3] Her greatest struggles are interior dramas too: "the Tempter" whispers lies of her inadequacy and faithlessness, yet the Holy Spirit counters with promises of affirmation and sustenance.

Amanda's continual prayers lead her to unexpected, empowering places. Faced with a vision of flaming letters spelling G-O, she exclaims, "Why, that means *go!*" and then she asks, "What else?" When a voice distinctly says to her, "Go preach," she doesn't hesitate: "Lord, help me and I will."[4] Before congregations of Black and white, men and women, Amanda Berry Smith stands up, often with legs trembling, chilled with fear, silently begging God for a message, and opens her mouth to preach. Time after time, she finds that her terror subsides, the Lord gives her liberty to speak, and the people respond with faith, moved by this most unusual evangelist.

Surely no one could have guessed that the same nineteenth-century woman of color would travel to India, Liberia, Sierra Leone, Egypt, England, Ireland, Scotland, and back to America. And yet this is what Amanda did, prayerfully powered by the Spirit to proclaim the gospel across barriers of race, language, and culture.

It was toward the end of her long life that Amanda Berry Smith penned her story, a difficult task, she admitted, for "one so unskilled in work of this kind." Her testimony to "the Lord's dealings," in which she mentions the word *prayer* 690 times, was written with the hope that her readers, and Black women in particular, would be led into God's liberating purposes just as she had been. She concludes with a plea that "the Spirit of the Lord may come upon some of the younger women who have talent, women who have had better opportunities than I ever had, to take up the standard and bear it on."[5] To carry forward the bright banner of prayer.

## THE WAY TO PRAY?

*Now I lay me down to sleep, I pray the Lord my soul to keep.*
*Angels watch me through the night and wake me with the*
*morning light.*

*Bless us, O Lord, and these thy gifts, which we are about to receive*
*from thy bounty, through Christ our Lord.*

*Our Father who art in heaven,*
*hallowed be thy name.*
*Thy kingdom come,*
*thy will be done,*
*on earth as it is in heaven.*

Threads of remembered prayers live within you and me—a line or two we repeated at long-ago family meals, a blessing received before our childhood bedtime, phrases from the Lord's Prayer recited in church. Now, in daily life, we may pray regularly—or we may not. But chances are we'll each admit to a time when we cried out (mid-crisis), "Help, O God!" promising to be faithful ever after. How about those occasions when, late for an appointment, we've begged God to reveal a parking spot? In grief, in hope, in gratitude, in fear, we've sensed our souls reach for the divine.

Across all times, continents, and religious traditions, people pray. Prayer is an act that is both familiar and deeply complex. Google the word *prayer* and you'll get more than three billion results, but I bet you'll still be asking, "If prayer is a communication with the invisible God, how ever do we pray rightly?"

In my Sunday school days, we were coached in the way of ACTS prayer: we started off with adoration of God and then moved on to confession of sin, thanksgiving for blessings, and, finally, supplication, by which time our spirits were humbly prepared to present the needs and desires we'd harbored all along. By the end of ACTS, we certainly had demonstrated our commitment to cover all the bases with God. To my fifteen-year-old self, it sometimes felt a whole lot like homework, just another checklist to labor through. At other moments, when my mind and emotions were in a whirl, the ACTS prayer gave me a place to begin.

These days I lean on the many eloquent prayers written by believers who came before me, those folks who somehow beautifully sum up my longings, hopes, and ever-shifting faith, lending me their words and their devotion when I'm out of both. Spiritual brothers and sisters like Teresa of Avila, Flannery O'Connor, Oscar Romero, and clouds of others bring me into their sacred conversations.

I collect written prayers that I find here and there, in old books, online, from friends. My mornings begin:

> O Lord, let my soul rise up to meet you
> as the day rises to meet the sun.
> Glory to the Father, and to the Son, and to the Holy Spirit,
> as it was in the beginning, is now, and will be forever. Amen.[6]

As I inhabit the words again and again, they begin to pray *me*.

Tradition carries me along too, as Sunday after Sunday I repeat the time-tested texts from the *Book of Common Prayer*, comforted to be speaking prayers aloud in the good company of other Christians beside me in the church pew as well as those past and future, across generations. There are occasions when the old prayers (yes, even of adoration, confession, thanksgiving, and supplication) that I've repeated innumerable times suddenly spark with new vitality. I sense the presence of angels at my side, envision all the company of heaven singing glory over me, feel the breath of the Holy Spirit in my chest. Other times, asking forgiveness for the "things done and left undone" brings particular failings vividly to mind. At the proclamation of God's forgiveness, my tense shoulders drop just a bit as the release washes over me.

It is also a gift to simply open myself to the love, presence, and action of God right here, right now, plainly, as I am. I seriously doubt that Amanda Berry Smith ever borrowed a formally composed prayer, except for the Lord's Prayer, which she learned at her grandmother's knee. Amanda prayed straight from the heart, speaking directly to God, unapologetically unfiltered, immediate, and personal.

Faced with existential questions, she cries, "O Lord, help me and teach me! I want to hear Thee speak!" Afraid and alone, she implores, "O Lord, have mercy on my soul! I don't know how else to pray." At the smallest victory, she flames with joy: "All praise to my victorious Christ! Hallelujah! Hallelujah! Praise the Lord!"[7] Whether she's down to her last nickel and needs medicine for a child, is elated after preaching, or is unsure about a decision, in every circumstance Amanda keeps up the nonstop conversation with God about matters large and small. She never stops to search through a religious volume. All her life and the whole of the universe is, for Amanda, a spiritual reality, and she's in the flow of it, moment by moment. How can you and I pray and live more in that unbounded way?

For a bookish (okay, *hesitant*) believer like me, Amanda Berry Smith is the exuberant older sister who pushes me to loosen up. She reminds me that prayer is, after all, nothing more complicated than "communing with Jesus" all the time and everywhere. As Anne Lamott simply states it, prayer is summed up in three utterances: Help. Thanks. Wow.[8] I can almost hear Amanda preach: Leave the dusty volumes on the shelf, shake off the stale childhood formulas, and get real with God right now—up close and personal. Pray your anything, she says. God is listening.

# TRY THIS

### Prayer Lessons

Spiritual traditions the world over teach widely varied prayer practices. How were *you* introduced to prayer? Take some time to sketch out your own personal experience of communicating with God.

- What is one specific childhood memory of prayer?
- How has your practice of prayer changed—or stayed the same—over time?
- If a child asked you, "How do I pray?" what would you say?

Now that you're warmed up, try praying through a prompt or two. (Remember: these invitations are here for you anytime.)

### Sit a Spell

The story goes of a farmer who used to sit in church for long periods of silence. When he was asked about this habit, he said, "I look at God and God looks at me and it is enough."

Take some time to try this practice. Find a place indoors or outdoors where you can sit comfortably and "look at God."

## Pray Your Anything

Amanda Berry Smith carried on a never-ending conversation with God. What might that be like for you?

*Connect.* Take a few quiet moments and a few deep breaths to become aware of what you're feeling and thinking right now.

- Can you turn your inner experience into a simple prayer, a few words directed to the God who is near?
- Write your "anything prayer" here:

_____

_____

_____

_____

*Act and Listen.* Amanda writes, "I asked, 'Lord, what shall I do?' and a voice seemed to whisper in my left ear, 'Pray for strength to stand up.'"[9]

- Is there a decision or circumstance that you're puzzling over right now?
- Might you use Amanda's prayer to ask, "Lord, what shall I do?"
- Close your eyes, relax your body, and take some time to listen.

**Help. Thanks. Wow.**

Amanda Berry Smith poured out *all* her emotions and questions to God; nothing was out of bounds. Writer Anne Lamott names three "essential" prayers that sum up human experience.[10] Consider crafting expressions of these simple prayers for your own moment in time.

- Help.
- Thanks.
- Wow.

**Borrow a Prayer**

For generations, Christians have written out their prayers. You might borrow one provided below or find a different one that you would like to pray for yourself.

> Great is, O King, our happiness in thy kingdom, thou, our King.
> We dance before thee, our King, by the strength of thy kingdom.
> May our feet be made strong; let us dance before thee, eternal.
> Give ye praise, all angels, to One above who is worthy of
>     praise.
>
> —traditional Zulu prayer[11]

> Dear God,
>     I want very much to succeed in the world with what I want to do. I have prayed to You about this with my mind and my nerves on it and strung my nerves into a tension over it and said, "oh God please," and "I must," and "please, please." I have not asked You, I feel, in the right way. Let me henceforth ask you with resignation . . . realizing that frenzy is caused by an eagerness for what I want and not a spiritual trust. I do not wish to presume. I wish to love. . . . O God please make my mind clear. . . . Please help me get down under things and find where You are.
>
> —Flannery O'Connor[12]

My Lord God,

I have no idea where I am going. I do not see the road ahead of me. I cannot know for certain where it will end. Nor do I really know myself, and the fact that I think that I am following your will does not mean that I am actually doing so.

But I believe that the desire to please you does in fact please you. And I hope I have that desire in all that I am doing. I hope that I will never do anything apart from that desire. And I know that if I do this you will lead me by the right road, though I may know nothing about it. Therefore will I trust you always, though I may seem to be lost and in the shadow of death. I will not fear, for you are ever with me, and you will never leave me to face my perils alone.

—Thomas Merton[13]


May the Lord Christ go with you wherever He may send you.
May He guide you through the wilderness,
*protect you through the storm.*
May He bring you home rejoicing
*at the wonders He has shown you.*
May He bring you home rejoicing once again into our doors.

—Theological Horizons blessing[14]

# ASK BETTER QUESTIONS
## AUGUSTINE (354–430)

*"God, where am I to find you?"* Augustine asks. He was a person with questions. *Many* questions. "God, how does anyone call upon you if they don't believe in you—or even know you? Can a person believe in you at all if they don't have someone to preach to them from the Bible? Or can someone know you simply by praying to you?"[1] Augustine's mind and soul were fired by the search to know, understand, and connect with God. Over the past two thousand years, seemingly infinite volumes have been written about this giant of Christian spirituality, not to mention the five million words we have from Augustine himself, passed down from scribes and calligraphers, on papyrus, parchment, and paper.[2]

Augustine's investigations range from the philosophical to the personal. "What am I then, my God? What is my nature?" he asks in his autobiography, *Confessions*. These are far more than intellectual puzzles; Augustine is staking his life on the answers. "What is it you are saying to me, God?" he wants to know. "What then should I *do*, my God—you who are my true life? Look how I am rising upwards through my mind toward you who are always above me. I am passing even beyond that power of mind . . . for I wish to reach you by the only way it is possible, to cling to you in the only way I can."[3]

At the heart of it all, Augustine's story is about seeking to ask the right questions in the right way.[4]

In his youth, Augustine was a freewheeling, inquisitive teenager, quick to ditch his mother's Christian religion for more sophisticated pursuits in Carthage, where he attended the Roman Empire's flagship university in Africa. A rising star, he excelled at philosophy, finished at the top of his rhetoric class, and headed for the glamour of Rome, where he landed a teaching position. Yet even as Augustine promoted the cultivated, tranquil life of cutting-edge Roman philosophers, his personal, spiritual reality was mired by guilt, loneliness, and addiction. Despite his success, Augustine wondered, "What good is all my nimble wit and book smarts if I am still plagued by a bad conscience?"[5]

Augustine's search led him to Ambrose, a dynamic Christian preacher who engaged Augustine's gifted mind and tended his struggling heart. Amid the intellectual wrangling, a spiritual crisis emerged as each of Augustine's questions opened onto another. Would he decide for God or against God? Could he relinquish his pleasure-seeking compulsions in order to come alive to life in Christ? "God, grant me chastity and continence," he prayed, "but not yet!"[6]

Back and forth he went, unsettled, until one day Augustine was interrupted by a small voice singing, "Take it and read, take it and read."[7] In the garden, in that moment, Augustine grabbed a Bible. The sacred words untangled his doubt, and he felt his soul liberated at last. In the years that followed, Augustine served God faithfully as a priest and then as a bishop—writing, preaching, and serving the church community back home in Africa. Yet he resisted the comfort of easy answers and premature conclusions. He continued to ask hard questions: What is Truth, and how do we discover it? Where, exactly, is heaven? What is the nature of time, change, and eternity?

To the end of his life, Augustine's habit of energetic inquiry created a flow of questions that moved him ever more deeply into God, himself, and his world. For all the certainties of his mature faith, he stayed curious. Augustine aptly concludes his

*Confessions* with the word *aperietur*, "it will be opened": an expectant promise that there is still more yet to be discovered in earth and heaven.[8]

## HOW TO FALL IN LOVE

I was only eighteen years old the summer we met. We'd been set up by two self-appointed matchmakers, church ladies who pestered us until Charles finally called, reluctantly, I thought, and we made a date. It's been forever since then, but here's what I remember. We met at Frog Hollow day camp, where I was a counselor. He appeared in a crisp chambray shirt, woven brown belt, and pressed khakis. I wore a hideous Freakies cereal T-shirt, muddy from a dip in the creek to retrieve a camper's lost sneaker. And most of all, I remember that we talked. Talked and talked and talked. About books, classes, childhoods, summer travel, school plans, life plans, good dreams, bad dreams. Faulkner, Heidegger, Jackson Browne, New Orleans. We asked each other questions: Who's your favorite band? What's your family like? Which country would you like to visit? We went back and forth into the evening, long after the campers were gone and the fireflies had come out.

Charles and I have been married for decades now, and I recalled that distant steamy July afternoon when I read about an experiment: a psychologist had tried to make two strangers fall in love in his laboratory.[9] His study involved sitting a man and a woman face-to-face, prompting them to answer a series of thirty-six increasingly personal questions, and then, in conclusion, having them stare silently into each other's eyes for four minutes. The first few of the thirty-six questions were pretty tame, like Would you like to be famous and in what way? and What are you most grateful for? By the time the couple reached question thirty-three, they were in deep: If you were to die this evening with no opportunity to communicate with anyone, what would you most regret not having told someone? Why haven't you told them yet?

Reading the account in the *New York Times*, I of course skipped to the end of the article. Had the two actually fallen in love? (Spoiler alert.) Yes, in fact, they had, bearing out the study's hypothesis that social bonds develop when there is "sustained, escalating, reciprocal, personal self-disclosure."[10] I am quite sure that Charles and I did not stare silently into each other's eyes as we were too busy talking. But we had unwittingly discovered that mutual openness that fosters closeness.

Influencers and experts urge us all to "be vulnerable," but it's not so easy to get there, armored as we are to curate, protect, and even defend ourselves. *Would you love me if you really knew me?* we wonder before we speak. Those Romans of Augustine's time surely kept their guard up as they jostled for advantage in the thicket of the empire's intrigue. Who could dare to be vulnerable when Caesar demanded unconditional allegiance? Who could utter a true thing when the rules of society dictated who spoke when and to whom, who was enslaved and who was free?

When I read the words of Augustine, written eons ago, I marvel at this writer who goes straight to the heart, an honest believer who asks a million questions and doesn't hesitate to speak his mind in *Confessions*. Here is a thoughtful guy who had his share of curiosities and queries. He experienced in his own body the restless loneliness that I often feel, the pull between faith and doubt. Looking back over his life, Augustine offered up a grateful prayer to the mysterious God who welcomes our querying. It's a prayer that we, too, can echo:

> O Lord my God, most merciful, most secret, most present, most constant, yet changing all things, never new, and never old, always

in action, yet always quiet, creating, upholding, and perfecting all, Who has anything but what you have given? Or what can any person say when they speak about you? Yet have mercy on us, O Lord, that we may speak to you, and praise your Name.[11]

Where can peace be found? Friends let us down. Partners break our hearts. Even the dearest soulmates are humans, limited in knowledge and wisdom. Augustine knows that only God can bear the full weight of our wonderings and offer us peace. As he famously says, "God, you made us for your own and our hearts are restless until they rest in you."[12] That longed-for peace is not so far off, so stay on the questioning quest, Augustine urges us; those who seek God *will* find God and come to sing with praise.

Still, isn't human love the sweetest of earthly gifts? And couldn't my relationships, even the casual ones, be so much better than they are now? While wordless, eloquent eye contact makes for a fun experiment, meaningful connection requires much more: open asking and deep listening. I often return to those thirty-six questions, finding the list again with a quick online search, and I pull out one or two to try with a new acquaintance, a friend, or one of my kids. It's a bit awkward, sure, but it nearly always takes us somewhere new. What is the greatest accomplishment of your life? Try that for an icebreaker. Is there something that you've dreamed of doing for a long time? Why haven't you done it? Even with someone I think I know well, I am surprised. Or I ask question sixteen: What do you value most in a friendship? Augustine would surely want to know.

# TRY THIS

### Question Your Faith

Paul Tillich asserts that questioning is an enabler of confident faith, not an enemy of faith.[13] Augustine was a person for whom questioning wasn't just a preliminary stage on the way to faith but an activity that remained vital to his spirituality.[14]

What role has questioning played for you? Think back to your childhood experiences of religion.

- What early questions did you have about God?
- Did you share these questions with anyone? What kind of answers did you receive?
- What did *doubt* feel like to you? To the people in the faith community around you?

Now consider your adult experience of spirituality.

- What private questions are you asking these days?
- If you could ask God anything in this moment, what would it be?

### Asking for a Friend

We live in a world of constant sharing. But with everyone posting all the time, doesn't it feel like we rarely ask questions or listen to the answers? In today's commonplace exchanges, try asking other people uncommon questions, even if doing so feels weird. Listen with care and then be willing to add your own confession (to use Augustine's word). You might borrow from the now-famous thirty-six questions! Here is a sampling to get you started:

- What would constitute a "perfect" day for you?
- Given the choice of anyone in the world, whom would you want as a dinner guest?
- When did you last sing to yourself? To someone else?
- If you could change anything about the way you were raised, what would it be?
- Can you tell me your life story in four minutes?
- If you could wake up tomorrow having gained any one ability, what would it be?
- If your home, containing everything you own, caught fire, what one item would you save?[15]

## What Do You Want?

Read the following passage from Mark 10. Picture the story in your imagination.

> As Jesus and his disciples, together with a large crowd, were leaving the city, a blind man, Bartimaeus, . . . was sitting by the roadside begging. When he heard that it was Jesus of Nazareth, he began to shout, "Jesus, Son of David, have mercy on me!"
>
> Many rebuked him and told him to be quiet, but he shouted all the more, "Son of David, have mercy on me!"
>
> Jesus stopped and said, "Call him."
>
> So they called to the blind man, "Cheer up! On your feet! He's calling you." Throwing his cloak aside, he jumped to his feet and came to Jesus.
>
> "What do you want me to do for you?" Jesus asked him.
>
> The blind man said, "Rabbi, I want to see."
>
> "Go," said Jesus, "your faith has healed you." Immediately he received his sight and followed Jesus along the road. (vv. 46–52)

You've read and imagined the Bible story. Now close your eyes and envision Jesus turning to you right now. Hear Jesus ask you the question "What do you want me to do for you?" How do you reply?

# LOOK TO SEE

## LILIAS TROTTER (1853–1928)

*Over lunch after church one Sunday,* two elderly ladies wintering in central Florida happened to mention the name Lilias Trotter. Miriam, the host, was intrigued by their stories of an unknown nineteenth-century English missionary in North Africa, and she began a quest that would lead her to find treasures long buried among the dusty back archives of an Oxford University museum: a trove of Lilias Trotter's journals, sketchbooks, devotional writings, and jewel-like paintings—hundreds of tiny pencil drawings touched with watercolor.[1]

Miriam Rockness discovered an exceptional artist who fully embodied a way of seeing God's world around her, an earth where Trotter found that "even the commonest things put on a new beauty."[2] Her paintings, drawings, and words restored at last, Lilias Trotter comes alive in her notebooks; on the pages, she often poses the question "Have you ever noticed . . . ?" She invites you and me to awaken our attention and see the universe along with her.

As a young woman, Lilias studied painting with none other than the eminent John Ruskin, who pronounced her "the greatest living painter," one who could "do things that would be Immortal."[3] Then, at thirty-four, Lilias stepped away from the path Ruskin imagined for her and followed the unexpected call of God to live out the gospel in Algeria, abandoning the wealthy, comfortable life of an accomplished artist in England, despite her frail health, others' disapproval, and no knowledge of Arabic; even she acknowledged it to be a fool's errand. Lilias loved the people and landscapes of North Africa from the start and ministered there until her death at age seventy-five.

Her commitment to evangelism did not diminish her dedication to art. Early on she wrote, "Oh, how good it is that I have been sent here to such beauty!"[4] And no matter the daily demands of teaching, prayer, and service, her artist's impulse to see and to create endured.

Living as she did in rugged terrain and spartan dwellings, with neither leisure nor time and without the luxury of large canvases, easels, or proper paint boxes, Lilias painted on the fly, often in spaces no larger than a matchbook—sometimes in the two-inch margins of lined notebook style journals. What remains of her museum in miniature features everyday created things, lovingly rendered: blooming plants, seed pods, bumblebees, and expansive horizons of sand, mountain, sunset. Bible verses written throughout complement what she sees with what she believes. Where her Arabic skills failed, she communicated without words; Trotter's portraits of neighbor children, women robed in richly patterned textiles, and Sufi mystics in white contain the deep affection she felt toward her subjects.

"Many things begin with *seeing* in this world of ours,"[5] the attentive artist remarks. Lilias Trotter did not paint out of nostalgia, diversion, or self-discipline. Rather, in lucid colors, she created a record of her spiritually saturated apprehension, of invisible glory threaded through the visible. God was revealed to her everywhere. "The desert is lovely in its restfulness," she writes in wonder. "The great brooding stillness over and through everything is so full of God."[6]

Many decades later, there in the back room of the Ashmolean Museum, Miriam Rockness opened up one of Trotter's sketchbooks and read, "Come and look. . . . The colour pages and letter press are with one and the same intent: *to make you see*."[7]

All who are willing to pursue Lilias's way of seeing receive an assurance: "You can never tell to what untold glories any little humble path will lead, if only you follow far enough."[8]

## WHEN I PICK UP A PENCIL

Will, Nan, and I arrive at the Met Cloisters on a humid June day, overheated from the hike up to the museum. We long to relax in the chill of the marble chapel, the quiet mystery of the medieval sculpture and stained glass, the silence of the galleries filled with illuminated prayer books, paintings of saints gazing upward, the Madonna and child. We find the entryway buzzing with visitors and signs that proclaim, "It's Garden Day! Activities for all ages!" Gathering our energy, we wade in.

Seeking the museum's flowering pleasure garden for a horticulturist's talk on "Magical Medieval Plants," we happen upon the Saint-Guilhem Cloister, an open-air courtyard where people perch on granite benches and sketch intently. A woman gestures us forward, offering us sketchbooks, erasers, graphite, and colored pencils. "This is a drop-in drawing session," she says. "Do come and experience the plant collection, both natural and sculpted, through creative drawing. I'm the teaching artist, and I'm here to help." I hesitate. But as the mother who always rousted her young kids to gallery talks, stargazing, and out for nature hikes, how could I say no to drop-in drawing?

My grown children and I find a place among the potted ferns in the shade of the columned portico. It's been years since I used a pencil for anything other than writing words and editing manuscripts. My inner adolescent mutters, "I'm terrible at art." After five minutes, I abandon my attempts to sketch a spiky desert plant. On a fresh page, I begin again, this time turning to a carved column topped by an ornate capital of leaves and fruits. I draw the vertical lines of the column (a bit wobbly) and then sketch the outline of a palm frond, a bumpy seed, a curled vine. I notice indentations where the marble imitates the bark of a palm tree; I add those in. Impatient as I am, the earnest artists around me keep me in my seat, glancing up, glancing down, glancing up, glancing down, drawing. The teaching artist speaks from over my shoulder, "I see you've captured the curve of that leaf," and I am bashfully gratified.

When Will, Nan, and I compare our creations, it's with pleasure and some amusement that we critique one other's style, depth, perspective, color. I know that Lilias Trotter would have smiled at our efforts; she would praise our willingness to stop and sit and draw the ancient sculptures that medieval artisans lovingly carved eons ago. On any other day, we would have walked on through this quiet courtyard, on to the next exhibit, event, gallery. But it happened to be drop-in drawing day at the museum, so we paused instead, to sketch and to see the beauty we nearly missed.

# TRY THIS

Keep reading! Whether you're a practiced visual artist or you never made it past sidewalk chalk and finger paints, there's an invitation here for you.

**Look to See**

This first exercise needs no tools at all. You won't even be drawing.

While you may not possess Lilias Trotter's artistic gifts, you possess the capacity to pay close attention to what is before your eyes. This was Trotter's way of seeing, and it can become yours as well. You can learn to be patient as you behold an object or scene, to linger on it long enough, tenderly and attentively enough, for it to begin to reveal its own unique nature.

Wherever you are right now:

- Choose something that is right on hand—something familiar or something new: an object, a view, a person.
- Set a timer and turn off alerts on your devices to create five minutes of undisturbed time.
- Get comfortable and rest your gaze on the thing you've chosen.
- *Look to see*, noticing, observing, resting your gaze on varying aspects of what is in front of you. Move around to get a better look.
- Allow your spirit's inner eye to awaken and your imagination to stir.
- Be patient.
- Allow the full five minutes to go by, keeping your attention on what you're seeing.
- Does the mystery, the unique identity, of the object or scene unfold gradually before your eyes?

After the time of looking is complete, ask yourself:

- What did it feel like to look at something for five undisturbed minutes?
- Where did my mind go?
- What did I notice about what I was seeing?
- Is there anything about this experience that was surprising or difficult?

- What have I learned about Lilias Trotter's way of seeing the world?

## Words and Pictures

Lilias Trotter often wove Scripture verses into her illustrations. Choose a blank piece of paper of any size. Write out an intriguing Bible verse, line of poetry, or quotation. You don't need to be an accomplished calligrapher but feel free to add a flourish or two. Here are a few sayings that might inspire you:

Each generation must find its own best ways of doing things.[9]

> Heaven is declaring God's glory;
>> the sky is proclaiming his handiwork. (Psalm 19:1 CEB)

God wants to show us that nothing is great or small to Him.[10]

I have been thinking lately what a work of God it is: just loving people.[11]

Now use the space around the words to draw or paint. Enter freely, even whimsically, into the meaning of the text. Allow time to read and reread, sketch and reflect.

## Draw as You Go

While Lilias gave up the prospect of a glorious artistic career, she continued to express her artistic impulse throughout her years in North Africa. Try on the innovative spirit of Lilias Trotter for yourself.

- Find a sketchbook, journal, or notepad—anything you have already—along with a pen or pencil that feels good in your hand.

- Take them along wherever you go throughout the coming hours.
- Imagine that you are like Lilias, occupied with ordinary tasks yet awake to seeing and capturing what you encounter as you go.
- Find objects to see and to draw: a coffee mug on your desk, a leaf on the ground, an apple on the counter, an insect on the doorframe.
- Are you in a meeting or a class? As you take notes, doodle an image in the margins.
- Writing a grocery list or a note to a friend? Add an illustration or two.
- Don't labor over these sketches; just draw with curiosity and playfulness.

# RAISE YOUR VOICE

## FANNIE LOU HAMER (1917–1977)

*How in the world did Mrs. Fannie Lou Hamer* come to give a speech on national television? A previously unknown sharecropper who'd grown up as the youngest of twenty children, she had been barely surviving for forty-five years, toiling on a white man's farm way out in the Mississippi Delta. Then, in 1962, Mrs. Hamer heard a sermon—and the call of Jesus to fight for civil rights. When the preacher asked for volunteers to go down to the courthouse to attempt to register to vote, she raised her hand as high as she could get it. Later she'd say of this impulsive act, "I guess if I'd had any sense I'd a-been a little scared, but what was the point of being scared?"[1] White people had been killing her a little bit at a time ever since she could remember.

The very next day, Fannie Lou showed up to claim the right to vote. By nightfall, she had been turned away by the registrar, harassed by the police, fired from her job, evicted from her sharecropper's house, and separated from her family. A middle-aged wife and mother, she suddenly found herself homeless and jobless.

But voiceless? No.

Mrs. Hamer joined the civil rights movement: a beloved community of liberty and empowerment, song and friendship. The effort would require more than aspirational words. Fannie Lou declared, "It's all too easy to say, 'Sure, I'm a Christian,' and talk a big game. But if you are not putting that claim to the test, where the rubber meets the road, then it's high time to stop talking about being a Christian. You can pray till you faint, . . . but if you're not gonna get up and do something, God is not gonna put it in your lap."[2] When her labors brought about pain, sacrifice, and persecution, Fannie Lou Hamer remained steadfast: Jesus himself demanded action in the struggle for human and civil rights.

And so this woman spoke out with her body and her words. When the 1964 Freedom Summer Project brought hundreds of college student volunteers to Mississippi, they were sustained by Fannie Lou Hamer's soulful songs, righteous rhetoric, and tactical action. Increasingly violent racism, even the torture and murder of co-laborers in the fight, failed to stop Fannie Lou and her compatriots.

Determined to stand up for people of color in Mississippi who were excluded from the electoral process, the group headed to the 1964 National Democratic Convention to demand representation. There Fannie Lou boldly spoke on behalf of her community in a testimonial that was broadcast on national television. Mrs. Hamer—once the girl forced to leave school at twelve to work in the cotton fields—delivered an unforgettable account of oppression in the segregated South, of her own suffering and of her neighbors' struggles. She was "sick and tired of being sick and tired," as she famously declared, and she would not be denied in her call for justice for herself and for generations to come.

Fannie Lou Hamer paid a high price on behalf of others, enduring personal losses, imprisonment, beatings by police, and lifelong ill health and impoverishment. In the face of opposition and intimidation, she stepped up willingly, declaring, "Christ was a revolutionary person, out there where it was happening. That's what God is all about, and that's where I get my strength."[3] The Voting Rights Act was passed in 1965, ushering in voting protections for all Americans. Mrs. Hamer and her beloved community had prevailed. While the journey toward justice did not end at the ballot box, the path forward remains illuminated by the example of Fannie Lou Hamer, a woman who raised her voice out of faith, love, and courage.

# EMBODIED SOLIDARITY

"Have you seen this?!" messages a college friend, attaching a shared Facebook post: it's a selfie of a smiling woman in a purple headscarf. I nearly miss it, along with the accompanying text by Professor Larycia Hawkins, a political science professor at the Christian college my friend and I once attended.

Hawkins announces her intention to wear a hijab throughout the season of Advent as a show of "embodied solidarity" with Muslim people. She will do it, she says, "because they, like me, a Christian, are people of the Book," a reference to the Abrahamic heritage of Jews, Muslims, and Christians. Professor Hawkins embraces the biblical call to "live at peace with everyone" (Romans 12:18) and goes on to say, "I love you with the power of the love that saved me and keeps me and bids me do justice in my body." Her post ends with the words "Shalom, friends."[4]

What a lovely woman, I think as I read. What a loving gesture. It's December 2015, a frightening time for many Muslims living in America; there's talk of a total ban on Muslims entering the country. Hate speech is on the rise, and ordinary American-born Muslims are threatened. I, too, fear for the women in hijabs, whose Islamic dress makes them public targets. Here we are in the season of Advent, awaiting a Messiah who was born endangered, on the margins. Professor Hawkins's act of Christian devotion on behalf of her community of vulnerable friends feels exactly right.

In the following days, I go on, preoccupied with work, family, and, okay, Christmas shopping. Meanwhile, Larycia's Facebook post has ignited a firestorm around race, Islam, religious freedom, and politics. The professor is put on administrative leave by the college's provost—a move that perplexes people outside the evangelical community, college, and culture. "What's the big deal about a headscarf?" they ask. Hard-liners respond: they reject the common theological position that Muslims, Jews, and Christians worship the same God and declare the professor's gesture offensive, even heretical. Amid the public uproar, protests in support of her are held by students, colleagues, alumni, and scholars. Hawkins declares again her orthodox Christian faith.

Then, under cover of an agreement to "part ways," the college terminates the employment of the first and only Black woman granted tenure since the institution's founding by abolitionists in 1860. Her act of "embodied solidarity" on behalf of endangered women has cost Larycia Hawkins her job, her safety, and her security.[5]

I've thought about these distressing events since then and asked myself, When is it right to raise my voice on behalf of another? When am I bound to present my physical self and pay the price? Gandhi once said, "Silence becomes cowardice when the occasion demands that we speak out the whole truth and act accordingly."[6] Hawkins was no coward. For all my discomfort and anger over her story, how many times have I, in my personal, professional, and public life, failed the test of speaking out the whole truth and acting accordingly?

Feeling unease rise inside me, I move toward explanation and self-justification. Sometimes the simple truth isn't so simple, I think. Sometimes I'm plain wrong. Sometimes speaking out won't make a difference. Sometimes I don't want to get involved. It's not my business. I'll deal with it later. It'll just make things worse. I don't care enough. My privilege disqualifies me. The other person won't listen anyway. It'll blow over. I'll say the wrong thing. Someone else, someone better qualified, will speak up. I'm afraid.

Speaking up, raising my voice—it's a thorny business. But I'm learning. I am seeking to face the real reasons I sometimes stay silent. I am stepping forward in new ways, learning, especially, from women of color like Fannie Lou Hamer and Larycia

Hawkins, each situated precariously at the intersection of gender and race yet daring to express themselves, only to be dismissed as threatening, defiant, angry. I borrow courage from their disruptive, countercultural acts of honesty.

Fannie Lou Hamer on behalf of her neighbors excluded from the rights of democracy and Larycia Hawkins on behalf of her vulnerable Muslim sisters—these two leaders expand my notions of community, teach me that my voice and my body are not mine alone. By God's grace, I am part of a family, a country, a world—and I possess gifts that only I can offer, including a voice that was created to speak.

# TRY THIS

Where to begin? Skim the prompts and then follow one that intrigues you.

### Speak Up

Fannie Lou Hamer and Larycia Hawkins publicly responded to specific political and personal concerns of their times, places, and communities. What does the present moment call up in you?

To get you thinking, sit down with a print newspaper and page all the way through it with an attitude of curiosity and openness. (If you have a complete Sunday edition, even better.) As you read the newspaper, pay attention to your inner responses. Ask yourself:

- What news stories press on my heart, mind, and feelings?
- What communities are affected by these stories?

- Where do I see myself or my community in these stories?

Choose one story for further consideration. Ask yourself:

- What one issue, cause, or question is at the heart of this story?
- What difference, however small, could I make in this situation?
- What single, practical action might I take in response to this story? Will I seek to learn more? Talk to a friend, family member, or teacher about it? Write a letter? Support others with a financial donation? Contact lawmakers? Reach out to others for guidance? Follow others who are taking a lead? Volunteer? Commit to prayer?
- Recalling Fannie Lou Hamer and Larycia Hawkins, how might I employ my physical self, my bodily presence, to enact my commitment? Where is the opportunity for embodied solidarity?

## Do-Over

*Many people, especially ignorant people, want to punish you for speaking the truth, for being correct, for being you. Never apologize for being correct, or for being years ahead of your time. If you're right and you know it, speak your mind. . . . Even if you are a minority of one, the truth is still the truth.*

—*Mahatma Gandhi*, Quotes of Mahatma Gandhi:
A Words of Wisdom Collection

Close your eyes and scan your memory. Is there a time when you felt you should say or do something but chose to remain silent or do nothing? Now replay the scene. This time imagine yourself speaking up and/or taking action. What plays out?

### Body Language

Watch *Same God*, the documentary about Larycia Hawkins's actions on behalf of Muslim women under threat.[7] What does "embodied solidarity" mean to you?

### Music Is the Message

Fannie Lou Hamer was renowned for her singing. "Ms. Hamer sang songs of salvation, songs of redemption, songs of struggle," one listener recalled, "and it calmed the people as they sat there on the bus, being intimidated because they wanted to be citizens of this great country."[8] Can you think of one visual artist, musician, or writer who is creatively speaking up for a community or cause that you care about? How might you support that artist in a very concrete way today?

- Will you share their work on social media, make a financial donation to their work, or purchase their merchandise?
- Will you help organize a house concert or art show, offer them tech or publicity help?
- How might *you* speak up through your own creative channel?

*Day is dawning upon us; the power of darkness is fading away.*
*From the true Light there arises for us the light which illumines*
*our darkened eyes.*
*The Light's glory shines upon the world and enlightens the very*
*depths of the abyss.*

—Ephrem the Syrian (ca. 306–73),
Ephrem the Syrian: Hymns

As I walk in the company of fellow travelers, they show me new things to notice and learn. Our conversations take unexpected turns. More questions and connections arise. Awake, aware, and growing, I am daunted too. Will I ever live rightly in the world? Dare I hope for wisdom—since perfection is so very far out of reach?

Relief comes one morning in church. As I walk up the central aisle for the Eucharist, the communion table is bright in the glow of stained glass. With the congregation, I sing a song by John Bell of the Iona community that asks God to "take, O take me as I am. Summon out what I shall be." The gentle insight arises: I am as I am. Human and incomplete. But God is here, the true Light who summons out what I shall be: ever more loving, curious, and expansive, I trust. I am, eternally, a spirit sealed and blessed and guided by the divine.

Throughout the universe, the Light's glory shines. You are about to meet six spiritual teachers who speak from across centuries and around the world: Ireland, Germany, India, Syria, the United States, and Spain. They teach us that *all* things are the means by which we learn of God, others, and ourselves. In their stories, they challenge assumptions, push boundaries, and teach lessons on how to lead, how to learn, and how to channel more of the Light. Open your mind to new insight, unafraid—for you, too, are sealed and summoned to what you shall be.

# EMBRACE ALONE

## PATRICK OF IRELAND (385–461)

*On the outermost edge of the Roman Empire*, Patricius, a wealthy preacher's son, lived in comfort. A skeptical sixteen-year-old, he really was not into his family's God and their Christianity business, and his Latin lessons were a drag. Then one day a band of marauders dispatched by the Irish king Niall of the Nine Hostages raided the boy's quiet village. Along with other plunder, they snatched Patricius and sailed him to Ireland, a Stone Age Wild West beyond the reach of Roman law. Ripped from civilization, ignorant of his captors' language, Patricius was enslaved by one of the island's tribal chieftains and forced onto the bleak Antrim hillsides to tend the warlord's sheep.

Way out there, starved, cold, and alone in the rough wilderness for months at a time, the enslaved shepherd did what many of us do in crisis: he prayed to the God he had long rejected. And an odd thing happened: as Patricius prayed, little by little, an awed love of God increased within. Without human company, he found himself praying up to one hundred times a day, even praying in the night and before dawn, in the woods, on the mountain, as he herded the sheep through snow and ice and rain. "I never felt the worse for it and I never felt lazy," he would write, "for the Spirit was burning in me."[1] In solitude, Patricius cultivated his energy and creativity. He discovered the Christ-centered spirituality of his family, a faith that imbued him with inner freedom despite his physical bondage. He even came to thank God for turning the direction of his life for good, for preparing him for his life's one visionary purpose: to preach the redemptive gospel of Christ to his brutal Irish oppressors.

The rest of the young captive's story features vivid dreams, a daring escape, a homecoming, a name change, and a startling call back to Ireland as Patrick, the fearless missionary who bested Druids, brought Christianity to fractious pagans he'd come (miraculously) to love, and ended the slave trade on the island where he'd suffered his own captivity. Looking back on a long, active life of "holy and wonderful work," Patrick would offer gratitude for the years alone; in solitude, the careless boy had been forged into a joyful man.[2]

# VIOLET HOURS

It is early spring, as I remember it, in our aptly named town of Paradise, Pennsylvania. My mother is in the kitchen assembling a pan of macaroni and cheese as my brother and sister tussle with the English Setter puppies in the garage. I wander farther, down the sloping hill into the forest behind our house. The woods are spacious and deep, though years later I'll return to find only a modest stand of ten spindly pine trees, another childhood memory downsized by the larger vistas of adulthood.

On that afternoon, the sun streams through dappling branches and onto the forest floor. The light falls onto a single deep-purple violet among the decaying leaves. I crouch down to pick it and see a second violet within reach and then, just beyond, a third. Close to the ground now, I pick a growing handful, one glowing violet leading me to the next until I've gathered a fat fistful of slender green stems, small amethyst blooms, and glossy heart-shaped leaves, a gift for my mother.

The word *alone* combines the Old English words *all* and *ana* to mean "unaccompanied, all by one's own self," essentially, *simply and wholly oneself*.[3] My mother and I still speak of the crushed bouquet I brought to her that day; she recalls the delighted pride I took in the abundance of wilted violets, the work of an hour, or was it two? I remember a five-year-old, all alone under the pines. There in the solitariness of my backyard wilderness, I was wholly myself, attentive, absorbed, engaged, content.

Those languorous childhood hours are now far away. Living as I have in busy households and preoccupied by a relationally oriented career, I rarely spend a day uninterrupted by others. I'm nothing like Børge Ousland, the Norwegian explorer who recently skied solo over more than six hundred miles of drifting ice to the North Pole pulling a three-hundred-pound sled behind him. After his extraordinary trek of fifty-two days, the tough guy admitted, "I feared I would be lonely."[4] To his surprise, he found that being alone proved to be the richest aspect of the entire trek. Like Patrick, fending for himself and his flock in the frigid winds of Ireland, Børge was out on the ice for months, in the solitude of his own body and his own mind, yet without the sad desolation of loneliness.

Much is made of the epidemic of loneliness sweeping the developed world, yet the word *lonely* didn't even appear in the English language until the seventeenth century. Loneliness—that inner feeling of being disconnected, misunderstood, emotionally isolated—has become our contemporary affliction, only heightened by a global pandemic, when the outward state of seclusion was forced upon us for a time, stripping away many of our commonplace in-person interactions with others.

But, of course, being alone and being lonely are not the same thing. One can feel lonely in the company of other people. And many assume that all alone time will be lonely; one study reports that an alarming number of people chose to administer a painful electric shock to themselves (!?) rather than endure fifteen minutes in a room with their own uninterrupted thoughts, separated from social media, texts, emails, and people.[5] What is it about *alone-ness* that feels like *loneliness*, anxiety, distress? Why do few of us experience physical solitude as Patrick and Borge did: as a time to be more deeply with ourselves and with God?

For pastoral, practical wisdom, I often turn to Henri J. M. Nouwen, the twentieth-century writer who himself felt both the pain of loneliness and the dilemma of solitude. He observes that we are usually surrounded by so much outer noise that it is hard to truly hear God when he is speaking to us. Solitude exposes us to an interior chaos that can be "so disturbing and so confusing that we can hardly wait to get busy again," back into our over-filled lives, where worry wins the day.[6]

All the same, Henri urges me to set aside a time and a place for God—and for myself. Can I recover that childhood presence of my whole self *alone* picking violets? In recent years, I felt this kind of alone on a hike in Big Sky, Montana, when I traced a path up through tall grasses and encountered a vista of Lone Mountain beyond. I've felt "wholly myself" in urban spaces too, as I've perched on benches in Central Park, lingered over coffee at sidewalk cafés, and threaded my way through crowds on Fifth Avenue: alone but not lonely. It's evidence that I can, even if it's just for a while, do nothing with nobody, all by myself.

Let's say I do seek out solitude today and forgo the distractions of the headlines, a quick text, a podcast. What might I find? Lots, actually. Quiet time allows me to unravel problems; my creative and curious mind roams, free to brainstorm. Solitude gives me a break from self-consciousness, that energy I spend alert to what others think of me. Alone, I discover space, maybe even permission, to explore my own thoughts, feelings, and physical sensations, a measure of courage to face my life and desires. As loneliness sidles in, I remind myself that I am not, in fact, on my own. God is waiting for me here, always, everywhere, with an invitation: "Be still, and know that I am God" (Psalm 46:10).

# TRY THIS

Whether you're an extrovert or an introvert, this much is true: to become "wholly yourself" in the way of Patrick, you must practice regular alone time. Though you may not be a polar explorer, herder in Ireland, or contemplative on retreat, you can still experience the tonic of the wilderness.[7] Moments of daily, quiet solitude wait all around you if only you seek them out.

### Alone 101

Does being alone feel awkward or even scary? Here's a gentle way to begin. Take four minutes and thirty-five seconds to watch "How to Be Alone," the Tanya Davis visual poem on YouTube.[8] As you watch, imagine yourself in places like a coffee shop, lunch counter, gym, or dance club. Choose one place you'll actually go and try out a new way to be alone. Record your experience here.

### Imitate Jesus

*But Jesus often withdrew to lonely places and prayed.*

—Luke 5:16

*Very early the next morning, long before daylight, Jesus got up and left the house. He went out of town to a lonely place, where he prayed.*

—Mark 1:35 GNT

Jesus was constantly followed by harried crowds, disciples, and challengers. He taught, healed, performed miracles, and preached the in-breaking of the kingdom of God; Jesus was a person of urgent mission and effective action. Yet for Jesus, alone time was no luxury to be enjoyed when everything else was done. He frequently sought out solitude: quiet places to pray, find rest, and receive clarity.

Those of us who follow Jesus are invited, too, into spaces of deep stillness, to places and times uncluttered by distraction. Even as we sit with our emotional stress or cerebral musings, the Holy Spirit is there to create, renew, refresh, and inspire.

- Take five minutes with a journal.
- Settle yourself into silence.
- Reflect on this verse of Scripture: "But oh! GOD is in his holy Temple! Quiet, everyone—a holy silence. Listen!" (Habakkuk 2:20 The Message).
- What comes to you as you listen?
- Draw a picture, write words, or just sit.

### Your Brain on Silence

Neurophysiological scientists have found that two hours of silence (silence being simply the absence of sound) caused brain cells to regenerate in the hippocampus of mice, the brain region related to the senses and the formation of memory. Freedom from noise and goal-directed tasks helps humans too. Time spent in silence calms our bodies, makes space for our inner thoughts, and attunes our connection to the world.[9] See if you can unite the quiet without and within and allow your conscious workspace to do its thing.

Put yourself alone in a truly silent place for a while.

- Consider a familiar activity that takes little or no concentration.
- Walk a path you know well (perhaps with noise-canceling headphones).
- Swim laps.
- Fold laundry.
- Sit with your eyes closed.
- Find a labyrinth at a local church or retreat center and walk its path.

As you spend time by yourself, let your mind wander through your inner white space, without music or stimulation to guide it, out of the stress of noise and into the healing of silence. If disturbances like anxiety and depression cause this to be too challenging, gently do what's best for you.

# REVIEW THE NEWS

## HANS SCHOLL (1918–1942) AND
## SOPHIE SCHOLL (1921–1942)

*Munich. May 1942.* The newspaper, displayed in a glass case on a street corner, draws passersby to read the day's installment of the *People's Observer*: a declaration of Adolf Hitler's latest war triumph, a rant against Germany's enemies, a slanderous tale of murder carried out by Jews, a scattering of brash patriotic slogans, dark warnings of world Bolshevism. Sophie Scholl, a freshman at the University of Munich, sees the Nazi publication for what it is: toxic propaganda fueled by totalitarian, racist ideology. "Designed for conformity rather than liberation," she mutters.[1]

Why is it that, of the newspaper's one million readers, Sophie Scholl, barely twenty-one, and her brother Hans are unswayed by the lies of the Nazi regime? The two were force-fed indoctrination since the day Hitler came to power; in the Germany of their childhood, only zeal for the "great patriotic war" was permitted, at least in public.

Yet at home, Sophie and Hans were raised by their Christian parents to have minds of their own, to engage fearlessly in open discussions, and to read books of all kinds, ranging from the Bible and Aristotle to Augustine and the Qur'an. Their father, Robert, insisted that intellectual ideas fuel action, preaching over and over the biblical command "But be ye *doers* of the word, and not hearers only" ( James 1:22 KJV). And he made no secret of his hatred for Hitler.[2]

Grounded in spiritual conviction and the teachings of their mother and father, Sophie, Hans, and their siblings were not deceived by Nazi power as they grew into young adulthood. Though newspapers and radio spit out a constant stream of lies, their eyes were open to the hatred and oppression around them. A conscripted medic on the front lines, Hans witnessed the brutalities of war, the killing of innocent people. Sophie suffered the numbing demands of involuntary Nazi youth labor service. They turned to a Jesus-centered faith that "starts when reason has reached its limit and one is forced to stop talking about resistance and start acting." When the time came, it was clear: "Being against is not enough. We have to do something."[3]

Sophie, Hans, and a secret band of university friends named themselves the White Rose and printed and distributed fifteen thousand subversive leaflets agitating Germans to oppose the tyranny of their government. The risks of their undercover publications could not have been higher. Spies and collaborators were everywhere. Paper was scarce; postage stamps were strictly rationed; printing machines were illegal altogether. Even possessing a White Rose flyer meant guilt. Still, in the face of the enormous stone wall of impossibility imposed by the Nazi state, the young resisters were determined to chip away at the wall of Hitler's stronghold.[4]

"We will not be silent!" the White Rose leaflets read. "Support the resistance movement" and rise up for "freedom of speech, freedom of religion and protection of the individual citizen from the arbitrary action of criminal dictator-states!" "STOP THE WAR MACHINE!" and "DOWN WITH HITLER!" blared their graffiti painted in black.[5] Within eight months, caught in the act of guerilla journalism, Sophie, Hans, and four companions paid with their lives.

Was the White Rose's effort to change German minds doomed from the start? Perhaps. But for these twentysomethings, publicly telling the truth went beyond success or failure. By their own reckoning, their writings declared a "very simple proof: that God is alive and at work, even in our time. You see, people need air to breathe."[6] And when the end came, eternity lay on the other side.

Sophie and Hans were executed, yes, but died undaunted. As the guillotine fell, Hans shouted, "*Es lebe die Freiheit!*" Long live freedom![7] Sophie, too, left behind her final declaration. The prison guards would discover in her cell, on the back of the very court paper condemning her to death, one word penciled in ornate letters: *Freiheit*.[8]

## INFORMATION OVERLOAD

Numerous times a day I skim a newspaper on my phone. The *New York Times*, the *Washington Post*, sometimes the *Guardian*. Five minutes to wait in a doctor's office and I catch up on the latest headlines. Today I read of illegal, toxic mining destroying the lands of Brazil's indigenous peoples. A hurricane takes out a whole town. A terrorist attack kills three people and injures hundreds. They crawl across the small screen in my hand, these graphic images of mayhem captured live and broadcast by spectators and reporters. From the door, the nurse calls me in for the appointment. I slide the phone into my pocket.

Alison Holman is a researcher who studies the effects of news consumption, particularly news of violent incidents. She finds that people who have high levels of engagement with media coverage are nine times more likely to report high acute stress than respondents who report minimal media exposure. Her conclusion? "I think people really strongly, deeply underestimate the impact the news can have," she observes.[9] Put another way: I need to rethink my habit of news scrolling.

Sure, I know that news coverage is far more than a neutral, benign source of facts; inherent biases, algorithms, and subjective points of view influence the content that I consume. And that's not the only hazard. From my waking attitudes to the content of my dreams, news can sneak into my subconscious and affect my life in all kinds of ways. Consuming a constant stream of news can activate the sympathetic nervous system, which floods me with stress hormones like cortisol and adrenaline, resulting in fatigue, anxiety, depression, and sleep trouble.[10] Yet I read on. As an active citizen of the world, I want to stay informed.

In that doctor's office, I feel a tension. I stay plugged into the dramatic news cycle, but what good is my engagement to, say, a poisoned Brazilian child or a family left homeless by the hurricane? Am I actually willing to take action, as Hans and Sophie did when they launched their White Rose missives into the world? Those two certainly prayed and hoped against hope that the German strangers who picked up their leaflets at a bus stop, restroom, or mailbox would be moved to join them in their struggle.

Alas, there was, in fact, no uprising against Hitler, no resistance ignited by the White Rose campaigns. After the guillotine, the young heroes dead, the Nazi machinery ground on, perpetuated by the Gestapo's fake news. The Scholls' sacrifices are not so different from those made by many journalists today. In 2021, at least twenty-four journalists worldwide were killed for daring to cover stories of crime; human rights abuses; military operations; and environmental, financial, and political scandals.[11]

In countries all around the world, covering the news is perilous business. Courageous journalists risk their lives to expose
urgent truths, and they deserve our support and respect. They
battle misinformation where powerful agendas shape what is
reported and how. We have much to learn if we are to live re-
sponsibly in the world, and I dare say that learning takes more
than a quick skim on our phones.

I take the news seriously, as Hans and Sophie did, and I am in
awe of their willingness to take action, which is where I feel I fall
short. All they had was an illicit printing machine, plain white
paper, a can of black paint, and no assurances that their efforts
would halt Hitler's war machine. Yet because of their outrage,
their bravery, and their hope, they did what was within their
power to do. It's no wonder the brother and sister are beloved
figures in today's Germany.

What about me? I'm no hero; I'm limited by bounded attention, time, and emotional capacity. But in memory of Hans,
Sophie, and other martyrs for truth, I have begun to think
more carefully about the sources of my information. In addition
to my go-to newspapers, I'm reading more broadly, thanks to
AllSides.com, an online compilation of headlines drawn from
news outlets across the political spectrum. I'm asking more
questions and doing a bit more research. I'm wondering about
what I will do with what I learn. Where may my attention—and
my action—be meaningful? At the end of the day, I'm looking to
discover what's human and what's real. Sophie and Hans leave
us all with a question: How will you and I make our world a
place worthy of one another?

# TRY THIS

Do you share my impulse to repeatedly flip through headlines? The next time you feel it, try one of these actions instead.

### News Tracker

For the coming day, pay attention to how, where, and when you are consuming news. Notice the stories that draw your interest, how you feel when you are reading or watching, and how much time you spend skimming headlines. Then ask yourself, In what ways is my news consumption healthy and helpful? In what ways is it shallow or disengaged from my deeper personal concerns?

### A Newspaper and a Bible

*Take your Bible and take your newspaper, and read both. But interpret newspapers from your Bible.*

—*Karl Barth (1886–1968),* Barth in Conversation

When you read the news today, choose one particular story that draws your attention.

- Read through it slowly, considering how the Bible might inform or frame the story.
- Consider one person involved in the news story and pray for them individually.
- Notice: Has your perspective shifted in any way?

### Plan Your Media Diet

Before you dive into your customary rhythm of consuming media, experiment with another way. Set aside a limited period of time to read news or listen to a podcast. Can you give the report your full attention and notice how you're feeling, where you'd like to know more?

When your time is up, step away and allow yourself to be immersed in the other needs of your day—the people and tasks in your sphere of influence. In the spare moments you might usually scroll, look for opportunities to engage instead with silence, music, deep breaths, poetry, or prayer.

**View from AllSides**

Browse AllSides.com and become familiar with their efforts to present a wider spectrum of headlines, opinion pieces, and analysis. What do you learn from AllSides about identifying outlets that use sound journalistic practices and avoid overt bias? How might this resource be helpful in your own habits of news consumption?

# TAKE A PAUSE

## HOWARD THURMAN (1899–1981)

*Nightfall had a particular presence in Daytona.* When there was no moon, the Florida night was darker than dark; it was black, Howard Thurman would remember. To venture onto the beach after sunset was to risk assault—only whites were allowed. Yet young Howard stepped outside unafraid. There the stars hung like lanterns, he wrote, "so close that I felt that one could reach up and pluck them from the heavens." For him, the night had its own language: "At such times I could hear the night think, and feel the night feel. This comforted me. . . . I felt embraced, enveloped, held secure."[1] In some fantastic way, the Florida night would forever belong to Howard, its velvet restfulness available amidst the blazing busyness of life. An inner place of pause.

Howard Thurman's grandmother, Nancy Ambrose, gazed up at those same stars during her twenty terrible years of captivity on a sprawling Florida labor plantation. Despite having every reason to fear, she was emboldened by the person of Jesus as secretly preached by an enslaved minister who proclaimed these exhilarating words: "You are not slaves condemned forever to do your master's will—you are God's children."[2] Decades later, Nancy would repeat these words to her free-born grandson, the sensitive child who felt a pulsing tremor of raw energy and that same sense of permanent grounding in God: the experience of himself as a human being.

Howard Thurman left home while still a boy because, for Black children, Daytona schools ended in seventh grade. Years later, after achieving grand successes in high school, college, seminary, and graduate school, having a highly public career, and with honorary doctorates and twenty-two books to his name, Howard would point back to his grandmother as his greatest influence.[3] Wiser than any professor of Greek or systematic theology, Nancy Ambrose demonstrated the religion of Jesus. Hers was an embodied faith that equipped Howard to face the world, encompassing all his personal, social, and spiritual concerns.

On a 1935 trip to India, Howard Thurman met another significant teacher, Mahatma Gandhi, who introduced him to the principles of nonviolent direct action, rooted in the spiritual needs of humanity. Enthralled, Thurman brought the transformative tool of social change back home, translated for Black Americans' own freedom struggle. By Thurman's telling, the ethic of nonviolence and the genius of Christianity, as it was born in the mind of Jesus (a person marginalized in his own time), powered a technique of survival for the oppressed[4] in every generation and every age.

Though Dr. Thurman himself was rarely seen on the front lines of the marches or sit-ins of the civil rights movement, his guiding, thoughtful presence was keenly felt. It is said that Martin Luther King Jr. carried a battered copy of *Jesus and the Disinherited*, the book Howard wrote for all "who stand with their backs against the wall." In his role as pastor, Howard Thurman sought to develop "the inner resources needed for the creation of a friendly world of friendly men" so that people "in the thick of the struggle for social change would be able to find renewal and fresh courage in the spiritual resources of the church."[5]

What then is needed for renewal and fresh courage? Howard offers an unconventional answer: stillness. A spacious spirituality. To people struggling for justice, to whom it seems a luxury to wait in quietness when the world around is so sick, weary, desperate, Howard says, "We cannot get through to the great anxieties that surround us until, somehow, a path is found through the little anxieties that beset *us*." To people "afraid of quiet," beset by a fetish of fevered action, he calls for *rest*, "lest we perish." Howard speaks of a "creative lassitude" that allows for the "physical and mental cessation from churning."[6]

Practical pastor Howard Thurman insists that sometime during each and every day, everything should stop and we must practice "the art of being still."[7] Even if it means that this time is snatched from the greedy demands of work, we must engage in doing nothing at all: no reading of book or paper, no thinking of the next action, no fretting over past mistakes, no talk. Little by little, Howard assures us, we will release our habitual fear of rest, of pause.

Howard Thurman had long ago perfected the art of being still as a solitary boy in his rowboat, fishing along the river, hearing no sound but the lapping of the waves against the boat, absorbed into the black Florida night. Later he would recall that moment when beyond the single pulsebeat there was a Presence who would always speak to him. In that intimate encounter, there was no voice. There was no image. There was no vision. There was God.[8] And there was rest.

## POWER NAP

On a ten-minute break from work, I'm cleaning the kitchen counter with one hand, eating a hard-boiled egg (my portable protein) with the other hand, waiting for the coffee to brew, and listening to a podcast. In the opening banter, the hosts are chatting about how exhausted they are. The one who's sleeping maybe five hours a night says, "I feel like every moment that I'm resting, I'm not doing something that I *should* be doing."[9] Yep. I'm right there with you, I think. While I'm up and alive, every moment of my day needs to be filled with something worthwhile.

The podcast guest is Tricia Hersey, founder of the Nap Ministry, an organization that calls people to claim physical rest as an act of liberation from grind culture, a tool for personal and community healing. The Nap Ministry creates sacred and safe spaces for daydreaming and, yes, naps, through workshops, performance art, and site-specific installations. In Hersey's training with human rights activists, many of whom work eighty hours a week, she hears people say, "Oh, you do the Nap Ministry? That sounds cute and nice, but who has time to rest? I could never do that. It sounds nice, but no."

I'm not much for dozing myself, despite my husband's endorsement of twenty-minute power naps. Set on caffeine, once I'm up, I'm up for the day. But now, as I finish cleaning the kitchen, I listen as Hersey, trained in both public health and theology, reframes rest as a spiritual practice. When you rest, you're claiming your identity as a person created by God, not just for purpose but for pleasure and flourishing too.

Rest is also an act of resistance, a rejection of the lie that your body is good only for labor, that old trope that if you aren't "doing something," then you're not worthy. Truth is, when you're resting, you *are* being productive. You're letting go of the stigma against caring for yourself. You're honoring your body with time to renew itself. You're giving your brain a moment to integrate new information, beyond conscious effort. To just be.

Scientists tell us that sleep is a primal need, essential for a healthy brain, muscles, immune system, and gut, and not just in humans. Bats sleep about twenty hours a day; wild elephants as few as two. Even jellyfish and roundworms can be caught snoozing.[10] One way or another, everybody sleeps.

But sleep is not the only kind of rest. Naps are not required (though they are, I'll admit, recommended). Rest can look like a long, steamy shower. Ten extra minutes in the sunshine. An amble around the neighborhood between meetings. Permission for a "lie down," eyes open or shut. The choice to stand from the desk, to listen to music. Time, wherever I am, to simply let go.

I'd like to be more like Howard Thurman, who slid into bed most nights with equanimity and gratitude. As a child, he was comforted to "hear the night think, and feel the night feel." He "felt embraced, enveloped, held secure," resting deeply because he trusted God to hold and protect him, despite the threats of his segregated Southern surroundings.[11] No doubt Tricia Hersey of the Nap Ministry would nod her head in agreement at Thurman's counsel to practice the art of being still.

Howard Thurman knows that you and I are in the grip of an addiction to buzzing activity. If I listen, I imagine him urging me to pause, to create intentional space and leisurely quiet time, long before my head hits the pillow. He prescribes a nightly walk under a sky gleaming with stars—or some moments of meditation before a flickering candle. He recommends a book of poems or spiritual readings, far away from the temptations of my devices. Certainly he encourages me to pray again, and experience the restorative blessings of aimless rest.

# TRY THIS

Might you give yourself permission to try one invitation—to pause right now?

## Pray with Howard Thurman

A pause is one powerful way to wake up from numbing routines, a choice to refresh and reset. But in the course of a full day, you may find that you hold on to your fears, ambitions, and obsessions, unable to step away from your activities or settle into moments of rest. Howard Thurman expresses his own struggle when he prays,

> Dost Thou understand what it is like to be caught between the agony of one's own private needs and to be tempest-tossed by needs that overwhelm and stagger the mind and paralyze the heart?[12]

Take five minutes to speak to God about all that you carry.

- What has you feeling "tempest-tossed"?
- What private needs can you name?
- What needs of the world and of others burden your mind and heart?
- What might you hear God saying in response?

### When You Can't "Just Relax"

I really hate it when I'm keyed up and someone says, "Just relax!" It is never that simple. On the other hand, I know that meditation, body scans, and soothing mental imagery can quiet the mind, calm the nervous system's fight-or-flight impulses, and take me to a more restful place.

Meditation is a skill that can be learned. Experiment with one of the many meditation apps out there; they are like training wheels for your brain! Check out Headspace, Calm, or the free Healthy Minds Program. Abide and Soultime feature prayer and Bible verses too.

Here's another idea. Get comfortable, close your eyes, and take yourself on an intentionally slow mental walk through one of your very favorite places: along a sun-warmed beach, through the deep peaceful woods, or down into a gorgeous canyon.

## Take a Break

Check out the Nap Ministry founded by Tricia Hersey. She declares that claiming the right to rest "is saving the lives of so many and saved my life. This work should be respected as a balm for all of humanity. Find ways to connect back to your body and mind. Find ways to intentionally slow down. Find ways to re-imagine and snatch rest right now. It is your divine and human right to do so. WE WILL REST!"[13]

What could rest look like for you today, even beyond naps? Brainstorm three small ways to choose rest and jot them in below:

1. _____

2. _____

3. _____


## Soak Yourself to Sleep

If you skip naps in favor of going to bed early, remember Mom's advice: bubble baths are the best. Studies show that a ten-minute hot bath or shower taken an hour or two before bedtime really helps you fall asleep—and get better sleep.[14] This works for a reason you wouldn't expect: getting out of a hot bath actually helps you cool down your body's core temperature, a key ingredient to great slumber.

As you soak, consider the spiritual dimension of caring for your body, recalling your own baptism in water, if that is part of your story. Imagine how Jesus tended to the bodies of his friends when he washed their feet (John 13). You, too, created in God's image, are honoring God's good presence with you and within you. And those bubbles? They just make it fun.

## Bedtime Release

As night comes, you might borrow this meditation from Howard Thurman, laying down your burdens as you practice a posture of trust.

> Our little lives, our big problems—these we place upon
>     Your altar! . . .
> We do not know how to do what we know to do.
> We do not know how to be what we know to be.
> Our little lives, our big problems—these we place upon
>     Your altar! . . .
> Pour out upon us whatever our spirits need of shock,
>     of life, of release,
> That we may find strength for these days—
> Courage and hope for tomorrow.
> In confidence we rest in Your sustaining grace
> Which makes possible triumph in defeat, gain in loss,
>     and love in hate.
> We rejoice this day to say:
> Our little lives, our big problems—these we place upon
>     Your altar![15]

# WANDER THROUGH SCRIPTURE

## PANDITA RAMABAI (1858–1922)

*Out in the untamed jungle of southern India,* Ramabai Dongre knew she was different from the village girls. Her father had chosen this life when he did the unthinkable: taught his wife and daughters to read Hindu scripture. Young Ramabai could recite eighteen thousand verses of the Bhagavata Purana by heart. In town, the neighbors judged it as heresy. Though the religious authorities deemed all women hopelessly unholy, even worse than demons, Ramabai's father, a pious high-caste Brahmin scholar of Sanskrit, dared to place the revered words of faith into his daughter's mouth.

Cast out of the community, the family trusted the Hindu gods to take care of them. Living only by "unbounded faith in what the sacred books said," they wandered across India, reciting scripture aloud at pilgrimage sites, surviving on the donations of worshipers. Ramabai became known as a Pandita, which means "wise scholar."[1]

But Pandita Ramabai's trust in the gods was shattered by the Great Famine of 1874. Though her family had faithfully fulfilled all the conditions laid down in the sacred books, the sixteen-year-old watched helplessly as her mother, sister, and father starved to death. Pandita Ramabai would endure even harsher judgment from Hindu society when, after a brief marriage, her husband died of cholera. Despite her independent mind and education, Pandita Ramabai could not escape the curse of the high-caste widow, her unchosen status that, by cultural norms that endure to this day, damned her to destitution and social exclusion. She searched and found no relief for widows within the religious texts of her childhood, no vision there to affirm her as a human worthy of redemption. The young woman despaired.

Still, Pandita Ramabai would write, "I was desperately in need of some religion, hungering after something." To her surprise, the strange Bible of "the despised Christian community" led her to that something.[2] One day Ramabai stumbled upon a little pamphlet in her library; it was Luke's Gospel translated into Bengali. Where had it come from? As she read it, it struck her as containing truth, and, ever the student, she determined to learn everything she could about the Christian faith.

Ramabai's academic study of the Bible took a personal turn during a stay in England sponsored by Christian missionaries. Visiting the Rescue Home, a haven "to re-claim the so-called fallen women," she was stunned. Why would Christians show such kindness to unfortunate women, those her own Brahmin community rejected so utterly? In reply to Ramabai's piercing questions, her host read a Bible story in which Jesus meets a Samaritan woman (an outsider in her own time) and enfolds her in respectful compassion. "I realized, after reading the fourth chapter of St. John's Gospel," she announced, "that Christ was truly the Divine Saviour He claimed to be, and no one but He could transform and uplift the downtrodden womanhood of India and of every land. Thus my heart was drawn to the religion of Christ."[3]

While the Hindu Puranas had grounded her childhood, the Bible ensured her liberation. Ever the freethinking daughter of a principled father, "wise scholar" Ramabai aspired to be at once fully Indian and fully Christian. She followed the Jesus who cared for the Samaritan woman; she loved the Scriptures that assured her of her identity as a person saved by grace and intended for good service. And as a linguist, author, educational pioneer, and social reformer, she had mountains of work ahead of her.

Ramabai created learning communities for needy women and girls in India, especially the starving child-widows cast out from society, desperate as she had once been. She learned Hebrew and Greek in order to translate the Bible into commonplace Marathi and then printed it at her own expense. She educated and equipped bands of "Bible women" to take literacy and faith from village to village. And when British clergy preached against women in leadership, she bristled, saying, "I have a conscience, and a mind and a judgement of my own. I must myself think and do everything which GOD has given me the power of doing." Newly "freed from the yoke of the Indian priestly tribe," she was not keen to take on the gendered assumptions of the imperialist Western church.[4]

A recent Indian postage stamp celebrates Pandita Ramabai and her pioneering vision for India's women. If she were here today, perhaps Ramabai would tack onto the stamp the motto of the girls' school she founded, adapted from Leviticus 25:10: "Proclaim liberty throughout the land unto *all* the inhabitants here!"

# CAUGHT IN THE STORM

Visiting hours are over for the day, and I leave the hospital, kicked out of the fifth-floor room where Charles lies, attached to blinking monitors and IV drips. I would have slept in the chair by his bed, but the nurse would have none of it; COVID-19 protocols are strictly in force.

I stumble out into the early evening light with no idea where I am. Countless hours ago, I followed the ambulance and ended up here, an emergency room with X-rays, MRIs, blood work, drugs, and doctors' varied theories on what had brought my husband to a delirium of paralyzing pain. Now the lab tests have come back with results: it's a bacterial blood infection that just may ruin Charles's heart.

I wander down Cove Street to its end, to a beach where the last families are packing up their buckets, coolers, and soggy towels and a yellow Labrador dives into the spray after a tennis ball. Our beach vacation looked like this three weeks ago, before the symptoms began. A low-grade fever, he had complained. It'll be fine, I had said.

The waves crest and crash. Barefoot, I hardly feel the pebbles as I walk along the shore, consumed by my fearful questions. Will Charles die here, far from home? I have to call the kids. What combination of truth and lies will soothe them while the doctors figure this out? Soon I'm on to picturing my future life alone, a widow in a house too large for one.

At loose ends and in need of distraction, I pull a slim book out of my backpack, *Pandita Ramabai Through Her Own Words*. I don't get any further than Ramabai's account of hearing, for the first time, the poignant story of Jesus and the Samaritan woman. Eyes blurred with tears, I can't read. But I'm left wondering, What might the Bible have to say to *me* right now?

I pull out my phone and earbuds and open an app of audio Scripture readings. I click on Play. A deep voice with an Irish lilt comes through, reading the words of Matthew 14. I know this one. Jesus has dismissed the crowd and sent his friends off in a boat; he is yearning to get away alone, to pray on the mountain. Next thing you know, it's four in the morning and the wind has come up out on the lake. Waves buffet the small boat, and the disciples are tossed about, awake and afraid. At the sight of a figure walking on the water toward them through the storm, they are terrified. "It's a ghost!" they shriek. Then comes a voice, a voice they love well. "Courage!" Jesus says. "It's me. Don't be afraid."

I pause and rewind, hearing the story again as I hear, too, the sound of the waves breaking over my feet on a different surging coast. Through the ancient imaginative practice of gospel contemplation, I experience a Bible story much like Pandita Ramabai must have, imagining herself as the Samaritan woman meeting Jesus by the well. I picture myself in the story—as one of the disciples. With those hapless fishermen, I have good reason to believe that this is the end, that catastrophe is here, that this storm will sink us all. I see a ghostly figure, and I am defenseless against its coming. The wind across the cove chills me to the bone. I smell the sweat of the men around me, taste the cold night mist, hear the howling wind. In my own imagination, the Gospel story comes alive again.

And then I hear that call, "Courage! It's me. Don't be afraid." From the Sea of Galilee, he speaks to me, the Jesus who comes down from the hills to accompany me in my tempest. A twist in my gut eases. I have met a Companion on this water, and he calls me to courage for whatever will come. "Don't be afraid," Jesus says, as he so often does throughout the Gospels. "Don't be afraid. Don't be afraid. Don't be afraid. It's me."

## TRY THIS

Pandita Ramabai's story may seem very unlike yours, so stay curious as you look over these prompts. What might Ramabai teach you?

## Put Yourself in Her Place

*I realized, after reading the fourth chapter of St. John's Gospel, that Christ was truly the Divine Saviour that He claimed to be, and no one but He could transform and uplift the downtrodden women of India and of every land. Thus my heart was drawn to the religion of Christ.*

—Pandita Ramabai, Pandita Ramabai:
Life and Landmark Writings

Here is the biblical account that changed everything for Ramabai. Read it now, with fresh ears and eyes of your own.

Now he [Jesus] had to go through Samaria. So he came to a town in Samaria called Sychar. . . . Jacob's well was there, and Jesus, tired as he was from the journey, sat down by the well. It was about noon.

When a Samaritan woman came to draw water, Jesus said to her, "Will you give me a drink?" . . .

The Samaritan woman said to him, "You are a Jew and I am a Samaritan woman. How can you ask me for a drink?" (For Jews do not associate with Samaritans.)

Jesus answered her, "If you knew the gift of God and who it is that asks you for a drink, you would have asked him and he would have given you living water."

"Sir," the woman said, "you have nothing to draw with and the well is deep. Where can you get this living water? . . ."

Jesus answered, "Everyone who drinks this water will be thirsty again, but whoever drinks the water I give them will never thirst. Indeed, the water I give them will become in them a spring of water welling up to eternal life."

The woman said to him, "Sir, give me this water so that I won't get thirsty and have to keep coming here to draw water." . . .

Just then his disciples returned and were surprised to find him talking with a woman. . . .

Leaving her water jar, the woman went back to the town and said to the people, "Come, see a man who told me everything I ever did. Could this be the Messiah?" (John 4:4–7, 9–11, 13–15, 27–29)

Now consider the following:

- What do you notice about Jesus's actions and words?
- Is there anything in this story that personally moves you?
- How might a religion of this Jesus Christ hold the key to the liberation of women or of any other people seeking empowerment?

## Imagine This

Reading the Bible can be so much more than decoding words or learning doctrine. Gospel contemplation is a spiritual exercise that invites you to envision yourself in the stories of Scripture.

In this practice, first created by Ignatius (1491–1556), you choose a Bible story and then envision yourself as an onlooker, an active character, or even Jesus. You allow yourself to taste, see, smell, hear, and feel what is going on in each scene. As you engage your imagination, you are able to spend time in Jesus's presence; as you are led down the path of discovery, you come to know Jesus—and yourself—more intimately. (The app and website I used to listen to the story of Jesus in the storm is called Pray-As-You-Go. There you'll find a whole section of imaginative contemplation exercises along with other rich resources.)

Are you ready to give Gospel contemplation a try?

- Choose a Gospel passage in which Jesus is interacting with someone. (For a start, go to Mark 4:35–41, where Jesus calms a storm, or Luke 8:43–48, where Jesus heals a woman with a chronic illness.)

- Focus your heart and mind. God is present. Be aware of your willingness to encounter God through your reading.
- Read the passage twice. Become familiar with the story and its details.
- Now get comfortable and close your eyes.
- Picture the scene. Decide: Are you observing the scene as an outsider, are you one of the characters, or are you Jesus? Where is it taking place? Who is there? What is Jesus doing? What are the sights, sounds, smells? How do you feel? What do you think? What do you say? Take all the time you need to imagine people's words and actions in real time and your response to it all.
- As you conclude, turn to talk directly to Jesus. Speak whatever comes to your heart.

### Wander through Scripture

Perhaps the Bible is completely new to you, or you haven't read it since you were a kid. Did you know that you can explore the complete Bible online for free? The Message is an easy-to-read version of the Bible, and you can find it here: www.biblestudy tools.com/msg/. Why not just poke around and see what you find—or what finds you?

# SURROUND YOURSELF WITH BEAUTY

## EPHREM THE SYRIAN (ca. 306–373)

*We children of the Western intellectual tradition labor* under the tyranny of logic and philosophy. For us, God is the subject of a great field of investigation, a problem to be solved through puzzling. When we have reached the limits of our understanding, stymied by doubts, questions, and our capacity to make sense of earthly suffering, Ephrem the Syrian arrives from the fourth century, an older brother who warns against the hazards of intellectualizing the great Mystery.

> Let us not allow ourselves to go astray
> And to study our God.
> Let us take the measure of our mind,
> And gauge our thinking.
> And as for our knowledge, let us know how small it is, and
> Too contemptible to scrutinize the Knower of all.[1]

Maybe, just maybe, the Holy can be neither framed nor tamed. God's incarnation in Jesus Christ gives a glimpse of an immense God, of a wildness beyond our heady theology. For Ephrem, only poetry is spacious enough to intimate the glorious truths about God—and to take us into direct experiences of beauty.

Ephrem's world was not always beautiful. A Syriac Christian born around 306, he lived in an era of volatile politics and cultural upheaval. He spent most of his life in the Roman frontier border town of Nisibis, caught between the warring ambitions of the two ancient superpowers, Rome and Persia. The people around Ephrem spoke numerous languages and practiced competing religions, from paganism and Judaism to early, shifting forms of Christianity. Ephrem himself spoke and wrote in Syriac, a dialect of Aramaic, the language that Christ spoke and in which the Good News was first preached—before the Gospels came to be written down in Greek. Ephrem and his neighbors in Nisibis endured three traumatic sieges, and when a treaty was signed between the Roman Empire and the Persian king, their city was handed over to the Persians as part of the deal. Ephrem, along with other Christians, was forced to flee.

Ephrem found his way west to Edessa, where he devoted himself to the church community in exile. There he set the mysteries of faith to poetry and music. He coached singers and prepared new believers for baptism. He formed women's choirs. He organized relief for the poor and the hungry suffering famine. As he approached the age of seventy, Ephrem—once called "the man of the broken heart"—died caring for victims of the plague, compassionate to the end.[2]

Almost two thousand years old, Ephrem's poems are filled with glorious surprises. He discloses a flourishing cosmos, both on earth and in heaven, infused with God's redemption. Where on the surface of things there appears to be only conflict, brokenness, and grief, God comes very near.

> Blessed is the girl He found worthy to indwell
> And also the town He found worthy to inhabit
> A needy girl and a small town
> He chose to humble Himself.[3]

Ephrem is so old that he seems new. Ephrem speaks out of his ancient, fourth-century perspective in images that refresh a calloused, twenty-first-century heart. Bees, blossoms, angels, dancing, light, seeds, grapes, lambs. Unbounded by the clichés of today's Christian radio praise songs, Instagram taglines, and coffee mug mottos, Ephrem's vision of God's overabounding love breaks through.

Ephrem's godly vision widens even further to embrace a deep sense of the interconnectedness of all created things, physical and spiritual. Where there is justice in human affairs, the earth flourishes. Nature itself stands as a witness to God, calling out our wonder and gratitude while challenging our arrogance and greed. If Ephrem were here, he would certainly grieve the present-day sufferings of the earth's people and environment, "the saints awaiting God in weariness and sorrow."[4] But would he put forth a theological argument in response? No. Instead, Ephrem slips the traps of unbending dogma and harsh logic with a spirituality that conveys the essential historic beliefs of Christianity yet brings them alive, clothed in beauty.

Intense contrasts of dark and light suffuse Ephrem's hymns, like the chiaroscuro themes we see on the canvases of Renaissance painters, where the presence of shadow serves to dramatically brighten the presence of light. For this ancient Syrian, "the Light of the just and joy of the upright is Christ Jesus our Lord," who manifested himself to us. Therefore, we have every reason to hope. He writes:

> Christ came to rescue us from darkness and to fill us with the
>    radiance of His light.
> Day is dawning upon us; the power of darkness is fading
>    away.
> From the true Light there arises for us the light which
>    illumines our darkened eyes.
> His glory shines upon the world and enlightens the very
>    depths of the abyss.

These are the words of a man who, even in his own time, was a vulnerable outsider, on the perilous edge of the Roman Empire, beyond the shelter of the mainstream, Greek-speaking church. He would die in exile, among the sick, still proclaiming, "Death is annihilated, night has vanished."[5]

Ephrem's life and artistry were sustained—beyond reason—by a beautiful faith in an ineffable God, a God of resurrection hope, a tender Jesus who came to earth for our sake. Why then be afraid?

> Creatures lying in darkness from ancient times are clothed in light.
> The dead arise from the dust and sing because they have a Savior.[6]

Logic will never contain the mystery of the incarnation. And so "stand up and be ready!" Ephrem urges. Let us open our eyes to the beauty all around: "The Light has dawned! Rejoice, O earth and heaven!"[7]

# CAN BEAUTY SAVE THE WORLD?

My friend Emily's daughter has died of cancer, and I just don't know what to say. Not "I'm sorry for your loss," "My prayers are with you," or my preferred Quaker saying, "I'm holding you in the light." Hers is too particular a human death, a grief unlike any other, too sad for words. Instead of sending flowers or a casserole, I take Emily a recording of the Requiem by John Rutter and the Cambridge Singers, a widely beloved Christian burial service performed by choir, orchestra, and soloists. I leave it on Emily's doorstep along with a note: "Listen to 'Lux Aeterna'—the final movement."

On the way home, I stream the piece through my car stereo, turning up the volume as I drive along the vibrant green fields of a late Virginia summer day. The slow pulse of percussion begins, and then the soloist, singing, "I heard a voice from heaven saying unto me: 'Blessed are the dead who die in the Lord, for they rest from their labors.'" Over seven minutes, the choir, harp, and full orchestra swell, peak, and subside with the shimmering light of paradise as the sun touches the tops of the Blue Ridge Mountains to the west. "With thy saints ever dwelling, for thy mercy's sake, may they rest in peace. Grant them rest eternal, Lord, and may light perpetual shine upon them."[8] Light eternal surrounds me. Beauty is here.

Writing about it now, I can only hint at the assurance that comes through the ancient words, Latin and English, and through the arc of the singers and instrumentalists breathing, singing, playing together, through the composer's work, written in grief over the loss of his own beloved father. This Requiem—like the services for the dead composed by Mozart, Brahms, Verdi, and others—channels grief, love, hope, eternity. Through music, Scripture is carried along by beauty to a place far beyond language. As I pull into my driveway, I pause in silence for a while, hoping that this music might comfort Emily too.

It has been said that "the world will be saved by beauty." I've heard the line quoted many times, and I'm still puzzling over how this saving by beauty works when there are deadly diseases to cure, millions of starving people to feed, horrific wars raging. What help, I ask, is a poem, a painting, or a breathtaking sunset when the earth is on fire? I have some half-formed thoughts about this. The vaccines against COVID-19 are beautiful in the way they harness the intricacies of biology and chemistry, invented by scientists who discern the elemental structures of nature. Strategists pursuing solutions to big global problems most certainly need out-of-the-box thinking: an artful willingness to imagine new approaches to intractable messes. One could argue that peacemaking is a creative act; true reconciliation goes far beyond rationality—to beautiful spiritual springs that heal and nourish the heart. There is an ever-expansiveness to the concept of beauty.

But today, after all, is not the day I'll finally answer the age-old questions Can beauty save the world? or What is beauty? Today I'm asking a different question: What beauty might I offer now, godly beauty that gleams on the other side of words?

# TRY THIS

Where might beauty take you today? Allow Ephrem the Syrian to guide you through one or two invitations.

## Step Out into Beauty

Ephrem's hymns, at once lyrical, ecological, and healing, make a space for believers and seekers alike—anyone who feels displaced, broken, or afraid. From his place outside the Western cultural inheritance, the ancient saint crafts a new prayer, one that starts simple and small:

> But remaining are all those things the Gracious One made in
>   His mercy.
> Let us see those things that God does for us every day!
> How many tastes for the mouth! How many beauties for the
>   eye!
> How many melodies for the ear! How many scents for the
>   nostrils!
> Who is sufficient in comparison to the goodness of these little
>   things?[9]

Prompted by Ephrem's poem, take a slow walk outside.

- For this time, let go of your worries and your logical thoughts.
- Activate all your senses to take in those things that the Gracious One has made in his mercy—the sights, melodies, and scents all around you.
- What is beautiful here?
- What does a fresh awareness of "the goodness of these little things" bring to your feeling and thinking?

## Recall and Relive

Find a pencil, pen, or marker and some paper. Sit comfortably and close your eyes for three minutes.

- Let your mind wander to a memory of beauty. You might remember a piece of art you saw, an incredible locale in nature, a song you heard, an act you witnessed.
- Take a few deep breaths.
- Reimagine the experience, engaging as many senses as you can, to recall and relive every detail of that beauty.
- Is there any way in which that beauty saved the world for you, at least in that moment?
- Without using words, draw a sketch of your beauty memory.

## Unexpected Artist

Ephrem devoted himself to the church as a deacon and teacher. He lived among the people, pouring out his gifts for the community— soaring hymns, poems, sermons in verse, and prose biblical commentary. Even when he and the Christians of his city were displaced by war, Ephrem never failed to create works of practical yet beautiful spirituality to build up his neighbors in troubled times. You may or may not think of yourself as an artist, but Ephrem teaches that beauty is everywhere. Why not share it?

- Where do you create your own beauty?
- Spend a moment considering your own creative interests and skills.
- What beauty might you create, collect, or give away for the good of those around you?
- Think of specific family members, friends, classmates, or colleagues, even strangers. What small embodiment of beauty could you give to one of them *today*?

Here are a few ideas that literally anyone can do. See if they spark you to action.

- Pick a few stems of plants or flowers, anything you find outside your door. Place them in a small vase, even an empty bottle, and leave them on a table—or at someone's door with a small personal note.
- Sketch a simple drawing and place it near someone's laptop, stick it on a mirror, or mail it off in an envelope. (Take it from me, mothers especially love this.)
- Create a playlist and share it with a person who needs some light today.
- Try your hand at a poem or song and give it away. Don't be shy!

- Think of something beautiful you could leave in a public spot for anyone to see, maybe something as tiny as a rock with a word of affirmation painted or written on it. (You probably have nail polish or a Sharpie nearby.)
- Consider something personal you'd like to say to someone, maybe someone who is hurting. Is there a way that beauty could help you communicate your care and concern?

# REPLAY THE DAY

## IGNATIUS OF LOYOLA (1491–1556)

*Young Iñigo certainly knew how to impress the ladies.* With glossy hair falling to his shoulders, he sported two-colored slashed doublets, fitted tights, and a show of armor in the latest courtly style. Iñigo's good looks were burnished with the flair of a bad boy; he boasted a police record for midnight brawling. Iñigo de Loyola was a nobleman hungry for fame, a soldier craving glory, an ambitious young man given over (he would later say) to the vanities of the world who dismissed prayerful introspection as the habit of more religious men.

At twenty-three, Iñigo grabbed his chance to play the hero. When the fortress at Pamplona came under fierce French attack, the brazen gentleman-at-arms urged his soldiers forward and led them into the breach, despite the force of the invasion and the certainty of defeat. Iñigo paid a devastating price for his blind arrogance: a French cannonball shattered his leg. In that moment—catastrophe.

Cut down in the fury of the battle, snatched from a life of restless adventure, Iñigo was borne home on a stretcher in humiliation and agony, back to his family's castle in Loyola, a pathetic invalid with nobody but himself to blame. In the silence that followed, Iñigo would face the toughest challenger of all: his own mind.

During his convalescence, the young man was tormented by questions. Who was he now and what could he live for, broken as he was? On the search for what he called "I know not what," Iñigo mustered daydreams of a return to valor in war and gallantry in romance, but the fantasies left him feeling empty, disconsolate.[1] Eventually, he turned to the only two books to be found in the gloomy castle: a volume of stories of the saints and *The Life of Christ*. As he read of the holy greats like St. Francis and St. Dominic, Iñigo found himself dreaming of a future he'd never considered before. He pictured himself outdoing even the saints in service of Christ the King, that sovereign even greater than the king of Spain, and in his mind followed a spiritual quest for his true substance and purpose.

He imagined surrendering himself fully to God—and this daydream fired up his spirit. And he took that daydream into the stories of the Gospels, imagining himself present in the scenes and participating in the conversations the Gospels recorded between Jesus, Jesus's friends, and Jesus's foes. As Iñigo placed himself right there with Jesus, walking among the disciples, he found he could hear from Jesus, and, it seemed, Jesus could hear from him. This wasn't merely daydreaming—it was intimate scriptural encounter and prayer.

And so, far from the battlefield, now consigned to solitude and stillness, the ambitious young man followed his imagination into his greater calling: a life devoted to contemplation in action. Outwardly, he determined to act as boldly as ever, yes, but his energies would henceforth be channeled by an ongoing, if unseen, conversation with God.

When he left the castle at last, Iñigo gave up his Basque name and took on Ignatius, an ancient Christian name for a man reborn.[2] He armed himself with the tools of imaginative Gospel contemplation: immersion in the biblical stories and ready obedience to the Jesus he met there. Wherever he went—as a pilgrim in Monserrat, as a student at the University of Paris, as a teacher of other God seekers—Ignatius continued to discover himself and discover God through a certain kind of conscious envisioning; through the eyes of faith, he perceived a lively spiritual realm everywhere. Ignatius meant it quite literally when he said, "All things in the world are gifts created for us by God to be the means by which we come to know God better, love God more surely and serve God more faithfully."[3] His message? God is already here, so you need only pay attention, ready to grow.

Though a dreamer, Ignatius was still a go-getter. He dared to free up a religion long confined within cloistered monastery and church walls and transform it into a Christianity that lived out in the wider world. Ignatius framed the spiritual experience in a whole new way with a method he called spiritual exercises, a guide for meditating on the Scriptures and the life of Christ that is still in use today.

Captivating and committed, Ignatius attracted followers to his way of devotion—companions who would come to be known as the Society of Jesus. Their action-oriented spirituality was powered by dynamic Ignatius of Loyola, that accidental visionary who became one of the most effective, practical human engines who ever lived.[4] The early Jesuits traveled to the far corners of the earth with a mission to help souls in both physical and spiritual ways. And though dark harms of colonialism would be done through them as well, through the followers of Ignatius, the world was changed forever.

If you and I also long to wake up to God's action all around, Ignatius's *Spiritual Exercises* endure as a hands-on guide, complete with a daily mental recollection called the *examen* prayer. We can join the generations of Christ followers who were willing to go inward and found themselves there, utterly beloved by God. We might even encounter our own true desires, make decisions informed by God's grace, and inhabit our own lives, day by day, aware that Jesus, too, goes with us. Along the way, there may be a moment when we think of a reckless, impulsive young man named Iñigo and envision, with thanks, the day he was interrupted by a cannonball.

# THE SELVES I'VE BEEN

When it came to defending the Christian faith, our high school youth leader was a zealot. He warned us about our atheistic culture, a place hostile to religion where it took grit to account for biblical truths. Skeptics were surely bound to ask us: Did Jesus actually rise from the dead? Did Jesus turn that water into real wine? How can anyone prove that the Bible is accurate? What's the deal with Noah's ark? Our leader wanted us to be ready. He handed us copies of *Evidence That Demands a Verdict*, eight hundred pages of biblical arguments to equip us for the interrogations sure to come.

The kids in youth group prepped like teenaged defense attorneys for Christianity, armed for debate in the court of pagan unbelievers. With detailed archaeological evidence, ancient eyewitness accounts, and logical syllogisms lined up on our side, we felt bold in our ability to protect and advance our faith—and if we couldn't give a solid answer right off hand, we'd look into it and get back to you pronto.

When I graduated and headed off to college, *Evidence That Demands a Verdict* did not make it into my suitcase. Arguments for the historicity of Eve and the scientific credibility of multiplying loaves and fishes held less urgency for me; my watertight propositions were springing leaks anyway. A philosophy major who fancied herself an aspiring existentialist, I moved on to different questions, and I took on the Big Ones: Who am I? What is the meaning of life? Who is God—if there is a God? What is real anyway? I favored black turtlenecks, quoted Kierkegaard, pondered my fate, and sought out wind-swept beaches. I squinted up into the velvety-black night skies with a hunger for cosmic meaning that felt far more grown up than the dogged demand for hard evidence.

College ended, as it must, and the reality I'd long puzzled over arrived—and to my chagrin, I found that it was composed of hourly wages and part-time jobs, maintenance calls to plumbers, grocery lists on tattered paper, an angsty grad student husband, and, eventually, three exuberant (read: wild) children who brought me to my knees, literally, to tie shoes and nurse bruises, late for work again. While tending to the quotidian, my mind wandered back through the questions of purpose, selfhood, and of God. Neither proofs nor poetics held enough weight to get me through my days, to make meaning of the cycles of playtime-naptime-bathtime-bedtime-repeat. Was this reality after all?

The arrival of a sixteenth-century Spaniard took me by surprise—and he came in the form of a small book with an unassuming cover. In the introduction to *The Spiritual Exercises*, I read about Ignatius of Loyola, that damaged soldier turned pilgrim, a human who lived fully in the world and gathered others to come along, dreaming and doing all the while. From across the centuries, it seemed that Ignatius had his own questions for me: Who are you? Where are you? How are you—really?

A hands-on teacher with a practical bent, Ignatius invited me to sidestep, for the moment, my endless intellectual wrangling and existential crises and to enter instead into practices of body, mind, and spirit. Spiritual Exercises? At first, I expected demanding disciplines: rigorous, predawn Bible studies, maybe intense fasting, thorny spiritual contests I'd surely fail. As it turned out, the only spiritual muscles I needed were imagination and curiosity. Ignatius prompted me to trace God's presence in all things, in all people, in all circumstances and to find myself there too, even amid the homework, sticky dishes, and tax returns—grounded in live, 24/7 time.

Rummaging around in Ignatius's toolbox of Spiritual Exercises, I came across an old classic called the *examen*.[5] Some call it the prayer of attention. Through this simple act of reflection, I am called to take time, often in the evening, to think back over the day. The *examen* practice leads me to notice those places in my day when I responded to God's prompting and those moments when I ignored it. I notice when I felt most alive and when I felt most distant from the Source of Life. I notice when I loved a neighbor or couldn't see past any need but my own. Since I've begun experimenting with the prayer of *examen*, it has created space for me to know God better by knowing myself better, even as life unspools, one day at a time.

I've always lived in my head. To be honest, I feel affection for the inner selves I've been: the studious apologist, the (slightly) tormented philosopher, the embodied nurturer. But of all the teachers I've followed, Ignatius has lent me the largest measure of self-compassion. He has freed me from the pressure to argue my theological case or to make the grand heroic gesture. Ignatius of Loyola loved Jesus Christ, he was saturated in Scripture, yet he was a daydreamer too. Thanks to the gift of his *examen* of awareness, I've found space and time to make meaning of my lived experience: an everyday life that glows with reality.

# TRY THIS

Ignatius did love hands-on practice. Here are a few actions to add to your own toolbox.

### Awareness Warm-up

What has this day brought so far? Create a few simple lists.

- What specific *activities* have taken your time?
- What *people* have you encountered during this day?
- What *emotions* and *moods* have surfaced in and around you?
- What words describe your *spiritual* experience today?

### Lost and Found

Ignatius of Loyola often urged his companions to "find God in all things."

- What does this saying mean to you?
- Can you think of one place or person or experience where you found God—unexpectedly?

### Walk Backward: The *Examen*

Ignatius of Loyola created the *examen* to be a prayerful experience, a mindfulness exercise for noticing signs of God's presence in embodied daily life. This kind of remembering can draw your day together and help you see the beautiful, complex patterns of light, color, and shade that God has been weaving through the fabric of your minutes and your hours.

While Ignatius of Loyola was centered on Jesus Christ, any person—believer or seeker, agnostic or otherwise—can find the *examen* a rewarding experiment in reflection. Some people do the exercise at the end of the day, while others practice it twice a day. A Saturday or Sunday can be a good time to review the past week and reset for the week to come.

Would you like to try it out? Here is my current version of the prayer of awareness. You take it from here!

1. *I settle down.* As I get comfortable, I allow some moments to pay attention to myself and to my outer and inner surroundings. I ask God to help me as I pray.
2. *I review the day.* In my mind, I recall the hours that have gone before, using my imagination to "watch" the day from start to finish, almost as if it were a movie. I notice what I was feeling, where I felt God's presence, and where I accepted or turned away opportunities to grow in love.

3. *I give thanks.* I remember gifts I received over the past twenty-four hours. As I slow down and savor these good things, people, and occasions, I offer my thanks to God.

4. *I make room for sorrow.* As I remember ways I failed to act rightly—or even failed to care—I allow myself to feel regret. I ask God for forgiveness. I ask myself, Am I being prompted to take some action to make something right?

5. *I borrow hope.* As I turn from this day and look toward tomorrow, I ask God to grant grace and peace—and to help me be ever more mindful of God's presence, whatever may come.[6]

DWELL

*Nothing is more practical than finding God, that is, than falling in love in a quite absolute, final way.*

*What you are in love with, what seizes your imagination, will affect everything.*

*It will decide what will get you out of bed in the morning, what you do with your evenings, how you spend your weekends, what you read, who you know, what breaks your heart, and what amazes you with joy and gratitude.*

*Fall in love, stay in love, and it will decide everything.*

*—attributed to Pedro Arrupe (1907–1991)*

When did you last ask the perennial question What is the meaning of life? Not of life in the abstract but of my own one life? What is my purpose? Vocation? Calling? These are weighty words with much at stake; it feels as if one's whole destiny hangs in the balance.

Five wise mentors are here to relieve the burden of making One Right Choice. Purpose is a process, they say. And they have advice: fall in love and it will decide everything. Design a life around prayer, work, community, and leisure. When the labors of your commitments overwhelm, get yourself to the beach. Be brave enough to do the unexpected. Start small, because daily intention becomes practice, practice becomes habit, and habit empowers your purpose. Dare to lead. Be patient. One is not a saint all of a sudden.

Know that with each sunrise we begin again. God has granted yet another chance to wake up, reach out, and go deep. We may discover, along the way, that we are dwelling in our very own lives.

And we are exactly where we ought to be.

# DESIGN A LIFE

## BENEDICT (480–547) AND SCHOLASTICA (480–547)

*The bell rings: it's the call to 4:00 a.m. vigils,* the first of the day's seven prayer services at the monastery. The period for labor begins at 9:00 a.m. and continues until the bell clangs just over three hours later, signaling an afternoon given to rest, recreation, prayer, study, a light meal. As the seventh prayer time concludes at 8:00 p.m., the community enters into the Great Silence, a period of solitude and sleep that lasts until the bell sounds in the dark. Another round of prayer, work, community, and rest begins.

Since the sixth century, generations of Christians have lived this regimen, cycling through life together according to *The Rule of Benedict,* a seventy-three-chapter guide to life in monastic community. It seems an odd lifestyle to those of us who resist the boundaries of bells, the sameness of routine, a countercultural understanding of time itself. Who could trek to the chapel *seven* times a day, after all? Yet some would say that this carefully designed life brings the best kind of freedom: the freedom to be finite humans embraced by an infinite God.[1]

Benedict, a young Italian who lived long before clocks were even invented, prescribed a daily flow of community, devotion, discipline, and service: an integrated life in which prayer and work are bound together, one a mirror of the other. He wrote it all out in his *Rule,* a spiritual and pragmatic how-to manual for monasteries, those religious communities he called "schools for the Lord's service."[2]

People who join any Benedictine community today must somehow let go of that contemporary urge to conquer their endless to-do lists, maximize efficiency, and pursue peak performance. From here on out, they will pursue *being* over *doing*. A Benedictine nun, asked to explain why she relinquished her independence, might flip the question: Who doesn't sometimes long to get off the treadmill, where many of us with full-time jobs log nine to twelve hours per day at work, sparing time for little else? The structure of her day frees her mind, body, and spirit; she chooses to spend her precious hours adoring God and living sustainably in the good company of others. What's the hurry?

Yet even Benedict got tripped up by his routines and best intentions. Benedict's twin sister, Scholastica, led her own Christian community five miles away. Once a year, it was their custom to meet at a farmhouse halfway between the monasteries, where they would spend the daylight hours together, praying and talking, just like childhood times. Late in life, as evening approached to mark the end of their annual visit, Benedict stood up to go. Scholastica asked her brother if he would, just this once, remain with her a bit longer; she felt the need to speak of heaven with him. Nope. Rules were rules, Benedict said, refusing to miss scheduled prayers back at his monastery.

As Scholastica bowed her head in prayer, a bolt of lightning sizzled across the sky, thunder rocked the cottage, and rain hurtled down in torrents, trapping the siblings there for the night. Benedict, shocked, asked his sister how she could dare hinder him from his sacred duties. With a slight smile, Scholastica replied, "I asked a favor and you refused me, dear brother. And so I asked the favor of God."[3]

Morning dawned clear as the two separated to take up the day's routines, little knowing that Scholastica was to die in three days. Back in his monastery, Benedict would see a vision of his sister's spirit ascending to heaven, comforting him with the memory of the unexpected, unscheduled hours they'd shared—even as the monk returned, no doubt, to the next ringing of the bell.

# TIME AFTER TIME

Once upon a time, my family's notable events were tracked on a Baltimore Museum of Art calendar, a monthly grid marked with our birthdays, scribbled doctor's appointments, the carpool schedule, summer vacation, Easter, and Christmas. It was an old-school pictorial calendar tacked to the kitchen wall, where I glanced at it three, maybe four times a week. I hardly needed it. Each day was heralded by the crowing of energetic children and ended a few hours after bubble baths and picture books—the bookends of days in which I was immersed, nearly always, in the moments of parenting. I vividly remember asking myself, What's it all for? The whole of my precious life was given over to small kids who would, hopefully, grow into large ones and then might have needy children all their own. I joined a babysitting co-op, found a part-time nanny, made space to teach some classes, yet time looped on, every domestic day a version of the last.

Our three little darlings have, in fact, grown up, and my pursuits have become decidedly more professional. Time has been restored to me at last—right? Now meetings, deadlines, and tasks fill up a calendar closely subdivided into hours, even quarter hours, from morning till night. Workouts and coffee dates are scheduled in too. The old kitchen calendar has been replaced by an online Google calendar, the tool beloved/hated by many, an indispensable scheduling tool synced across my devices.

Morning brings another day of work. Before my feet hit the floor, a detailed email awaits, subject line: Daily Agenda for Karen Marsh as of 5 a.m. My heart speeds up just a beat. Plans are shared virtually with my work colleagues. I'm sent automated text notifications and reminders by email as the day ticks by. I struggle constantly to track myself in space, no longer grounded by toddlers at my knee. Where am I expected to be in a given moment—in person, on Zoom, on the phone?

Philosophers, bosses, and grandmothers have said all kinds of things about time, how it waits for no one, how it flies, how we waste it, how we should make the most of it. By Shakespeare's frank reckoning, there's simply "Tomorrow, and tomorrow, and tomorrow" and then it's "Out, out, brief candle!"[4] The time I get on this earth is the time I get, and there's no creating more of it; mastery of the clock is an illusion. The more I fight the truth of the situation, the more rushed, impatient, and overwhelmed I feel.[5] Seriously: Why did I ever think that time was all mine to save or to spend?

The psalmist turns toward God with his prayer, "My times are in your hands" (Psalm 31:15). I sure hope so, because I can't manage this thing on my own.

I've been reading Benedict again. For all his detailed routines and monastic regimens (not for me, I murmur), Benedict is on to something true: only by taking my life apart from time to time, examining it honestly and then putting it back together thoughtfully and prayerfully, can I have some measure of confidence that I am living the life I was meant to lead.[6] Am I brave enough to do that?

I've made some adjustments. These days I put off the review of that daily agenda waiting in my inbox. I stumble down to the kitchen, make a cup of coffee, and sit by the window that overlooks the garden. I listen to a brief Scripture podcast[7] and take several deep breaths, allowing myself time to notice a cardinal in the holly tree. There is no rushing the sunrise. These brief, protected moments bring me into an awareness of the presence of God, whose time is eternal, unending, unspooling, generously extravagant. My times are in God's hands, and I have all the time I need.

# TRY THIS

Here are several experiments with time. Choose one or more and design a new kind of day.

### Pray Your Day

Benedict and his community remind us that our time is in God's hands. And that is good news. Can you practice believing this for yourself?

Get comfortable and take a few relaxed breaths. Sit with this prayer of release for the day to come:

> This is another day, O Lord. I know not what it will bring forth, but make me ready, Lord, for whatever it may be. If I am to stand up, help me to stand bravely. If I am to sit still, help me to sit quietly. If I am to lie low, help me do it patiently. And if I am to do nothing, let me do it gallantly. Make these words more than words, and give me the Spirit of Jesus. Amen.[8]

### "Have a Good Day!"

Benedict begins his *Rule* with these words: "Seeking his workers in a multitude of people, the Lord calls out and lifts His voice again: Is there anyone here who yearns for life and desires to see good days?"[9] What does a good day look like for you? Consider your own optimal balance of rest and play, time with others, work, and prayer. Now try this: write out a schedule for the next twenty-four hours, including the plans already on the books. As you block in the hours, look for any openings, however small, where you could make a choice to bring your day more into line with your ideal "good day"?

### Get Real with Your Rule

Benedict and his community followed an explicit rule of life. What's *your* rule of life? If the idea that you, too, live by a rule feels strange, ask yourself (honestly) how you spend your time, day by day, hour by hour. What probably unwritten rule drives your commitments and habits?

To dig deeper, look at your calendar from the past week. Take seven minutes to write down snapshots of the past seven days as you lived them, filling in detail where you can.

- Sunday
- Monday
- Tuesday
- Wednesday
- Thursday
- Friday
- Saturday

Now ask yourself:

- What activities took up the largest chunks of my time?
- What people, commitments, or habits had the greatest power over my schedule?
- Where did I pay attention to God throughout my week?
- What hoped-for activities or practices were missing from my week?
- How would I describe my rule of life as I am living life now?

# CHOOSE YOUR INTENTION
## BROTHER LAWRENCE (1614–1691)

*Down in the steamy kitchen,* Brother Lawrence tended fires, la-dled soup, baked bread, scrubbed potatoes, balanced platters, and scoured cauldrons, ever at the bidding of the monastery from dawn to dusk. Despite the demands and distractions, this disabled, barely literate peasant held on to one daily focus: to remain aware of God's presence. His focus became so clear that he was happy to "pick up a straw from the ground for love of God, seeking Him only, and nothing else."[1] In his own time, this servant to the Servants of God drew a stream of people who sought his counsel and comfort. Today Brother Lawrence's practice of the presence of God still resonates with those of us who struggle to get through the day with some sense of intention.

"One is not a saint all of a sudden," Brother Lawrence would say gently; he himself had come into his spiritual confidence the hard way.[2] When he'd signed on at the Paris monastery, he'd been assigned to kitchen duty—a hot, unpleasant gig he hated, but what else could he do, unskilled and uneducated as he was? After frustrating years striving to master the theological doc-trines and complex rituals of the church, Brother Lawrence fi-nally discovered his own particular way to worship God. Even as he bustled about his usual occupations right there in the base-ment scullery, he determined to pursue one single purpose: to go through each day and every hour with a moment-by-moment attention to God.[3]

This is what Brother Lawrence did. Whenever his mind wandered from God's loving presence, he resolved to begin anew, picking himself up after his falls, doing small acts of faith and love, returning himself to his conversation with God with words of recommitment, saying, "Lord, work with me; receive my work and possess all my affections."[4] Over time, Brother Lawrence's intention became practice; practice became habit; habit became an ongoing conversation with God.

Brother Lawrence cultivated not just a relationship with God; his relationships with other people flourished too. All manner of sophisticated and esteemed visitors, from monks, bishops, and priests to high-ranking women of church and court, were drawn to this unlikely counselor in the kitchen. Once you got past his rough exterior, people marveled to each other, you discovered unusual wisdom, an inner freedom, and a cheerful, open manner. Brother Lawrence brought out confidences. You felt as if you could tell the man absolutely anything.

To each person, the lay brother dispensed pretty much the same advice. Simply love God, whoever you may be. Brother Lawrence urged an ordinary, sustaining spirituality: the practice of the presence of God amid everyday distractions. Anyone could do it. Even a military man, in the moment of racing into battle with drawn sword, could offer "a brief, little remembrance" of God. "The business and commerce of the world cannot serve as an excuse for neglecting our duty," he declared. "God is everywhere. We can speak to Him where ever we are. Our hearts can speak to Him in a thousand different ways. All we need is a little love, and then living this way will not be difficult."[5] Only an intention would be needed—a wish to keep company with God, the loving One who is so close at hand, just waiting to be noticed.

# POST-IT PRAYERS

"Take this cream and massage it into the scar seven times a day." The dermatologist handed me the ointment to treat the pink pucker between my eyebrows, evidence of a recent surgery to remove skin cancer. As I stood to go, Dr. Olsen added, "I'm serious. Apply it *religiously*."

Out the door I went, back into a day of phone calls, emails, projects, the usual. That night, brushing my teeth, I glanced in the mirror, and there was the jagged scar. I had not thought to massage it even once; the ointment was still in my backpack. I dug out the medicine, dipped in my finger, and rubbed it onto my forehead. A sensation came back to me then: the memory of a priest anointing me just there, the perfumed scent of olive oil and balsam, and the words, "Karen, you are sealed by the Holy Spirit and marked as Christ's own forever." There at the sink, my place of injury recalled a place of blessing, baptism, reassurance.

A new habit calls for an old trick: sticky notes. On my computer monitor, bathroom mirror, car dashboard, tiny flags remind me to do small, simple things, typically in the form of stern commands: "Call Mom!" "Drink 8 oz water NOW!" "Posture!" The dermatologist's instruction to massage that scar *religiously* and the baptismal memory gave me an idea. I opted for larger sticky notes and wrote the verse "God, your God, has anointed you with the oil of gladness" (Psalm 45:7 RSV) on four of them. Stuck around the house, the notes have become a gentler prompt toward my healing *as directed*. The words of the psalmist in mind, I often reach for the prescription ointment there by the kitchen sink. Yes, I think, as I feel the pressure on my forehead, I want that holy medicine of gladness too.

Brother Lawrence would approve of the sticky note method. He urged novices like me to listen often—to listen for God and listen for our own souls—each day, however filled with other occupations. Brother Lawrence, the deeply prayerful guy whose inner life flourished amidst his own kitchen chaos, always started small, holding off on grand resolutions in favor of humble gestures, beginnings, experiments. He had a strong practical side. He knew that our best intentions, from scar massages to small prayers, need some version of that Post-it note to return our attention to the practice of the presence of God. In monasteries, the bell rings everyone to prayer; far from the resonant chimes of the abbey, you and I are left to create our own cues.

Lately, I've begun to add something new to my routine. In the spirit of Brother Lawrence's practice, I choose a particular intention for each new day. A hope, an anchor, a prayer. Morning is the obvious time to set an intention; this is nothing original, of course. Throughout the centuries, Jews and Muslims alike have celebrated every dawn as another new start, a clean slate. For Christians, it's yet another resurrection.

While the coffee is still hot and before I'm smothered in emails and texts, I take a moment to write a few words that express my micro commitment—words that I plan to take along the way. Some people call this a mantra, borrowing from the Sanskrit. I prefer the word *antiphon*: a tiny prayer crafted from a fragment of Scripture, a phrase from poetry, or even my imagination. The purpose of the intention, the antiphon, is to tap in to something inside myself, something I can reach for even in disruption, noise, and activity.[6] To help me toward deep listening for God, for myself.

Besides the fallback Post-it, I've sometimes kept a smooth chestnut or a colored pebble in my pocket as a prompt. I've also used actions as my cue: when I wash my hands, when I'm at a red light, when I check my text messages, when I see a tree, I am reminded to breathe the day's antiphon, those simple words that return me to my intention. On one day, it's "Be not afraid" or "Lord, have mercy," on another, "I am the beloved." Another fragment comes from Psalm 23:6: "Surely goodness and mercy shall follow me" (KJV).

It all seems quite simple when Brother Lawrence explains it. He says, "You do not need to shout out loud. God is closer than we think," nudging us with the Spirit's promptings. "Everyone is capable of these familiar conversations with God—some more, some less. God knows what our capabilities are." The good brother's words invite me into a fresh morning: "Let us begin, for perhaps God is only awaiting a generous resolve on our part. Take courage."[7]

# TRY THIS

Start small. Choose one prompt inspired by Brother Lawrence.

### Make It and Take It

Pause to listen: What is your hope or desire right now?

- Choose one intention for this day.
- Select (or create) an antiphon, a small utterance, that encapsulates your intention.
- Let your antiphon or mantra be uncomplicated.
- Write out your antiphon and place it somewhere you will see it and return to your intention amid your activities.
- Allow your antiphon to become an ongoing meditation on God's loving presence with you.

Here are a few antiphons to get you started:

> By the grace of God I am loved, I am forgiven, I am cared for.
>
> I take refuge in you, LORD, my God. (Ps. 7:1 CEB)
>
> I need only courage and willingness. (Brother Lawrence)[8]
>
> Holy One of blessing, Your presence fills the universe. Your presence fills me. (Lawrence Kushner)[9]
>
> i thank You God for most this amazing day. (e. e. cummings)[10]
>
> Hide me in the shadow of your wings. (Ps. 17:8)
>
> My crown has been bought and paid for. All I have to do is wear it. (James Baldwin)[11]
>
> Conscious breathing is my anchor. (Thich Nhat Hanh)[12]
>
> I resolve to begin anew to remain with God as if I had never strayed. (Brother Lawrence)[13]

## For the Love

*We must not grow weary of doing little things for the love of God, who looks not on the great size of the work, but on the love of it.*

—Brother Lawrence, Practicing the Presence of God

Might you think of one thing you can do in the coming twenty-four hours for the sake of God or someone else? Put aside grand resolutions for now; settle on a small, practical action that expresses your care. Make a concrete plan to act on your intention.

## Practice Makes . . . ?

*Become accustomed little by little to adore God in this way: ask God for grace; offer God your heart from time to time during the day in the midst of your work, at every moment if you can. Do not burden yourself with rules or particular devotions but act with faith, with humility and with love. . . . We must not be surprised at failing frequently in the beginning; in the end, we will have developed the habit that enables us to produce acts of love without thinking about them, and derive a great deal of pleasure from them.*

—Brother Lawrence, Practicing the Presence of God

Brother Lawrence's spirituality requires no secret prayers, complex strategies, or special knowledge—only an ongoing, mindful awareness of God's presence. Still, he's realistic about the process of getting there.

Brother Lawrence would agree with current behavioral experts who teach that tiny is mighty when it comes to change. Though they might feel insignificant, small steps allow you to gain the momentum you need to reach sustainable goals.[14] Whatever the outcome, faith, hope, and love eventually carry the day.

Consider your own experience.

- Identify one positive habit that is engrained in your daily life.
- How and when did you form this habit?
- What was difficult about establishing the habit?
- What tiny steps were key to forming this positive habit?
- What is one reward that you enjoy, thanks to this habit?
- What is one new habit that you'd like to develop?

## Sticky Wisdom

Read the following words from Brother Lawrence. If one of the quotations challenges or inspires you, write it down on a sticky note.

Let God do with me as God wishes, I desire only God and to be wholly God's.

In the midst of your troubles take comfort in God as often as you can.

One need not cry out very loudly; God is nearer to you than you think.

The least little remembrance will always be pleasing to God.

This sums up our entire call and duty, friends: to adore God and to love God, without worrying about the rest.[15]

Post the note in your kitchen, where you'll be reminded of the old servant to the Servants of God.

# DO THE UNEXPECTED

## FRANCIS OF ASSISI (1181–1226) AND CLARE OF ASSISI (1194–1250)

*The Bernardones had high hopes for their expected child,* one destined to expand the family's international textile enterprise and boost their standing in Assisi's wealthy society. As it happened, Pietro was far away on business when the baby was born, leaving the infant's naming and christening to his wife, Pica. She called him Francis, affectionately referring to him as Frenchy— her golden boy, her precious one. When Pica swaddled her newborn in soft white linen and lamb's wool, she couldn't have imagined what was to come. Francis would reject it all—the comfortable home, luxurious clothing, lucrative career—for a precarious existence in the wild. Instead of linen and wool, Francis would choose rough burlap and bare feet. All for the love of God.

As he grew, all was well with cheerful Francis Bernardone. He caroused, carefree, with his pals, ever secure in the assurance of a respectable marriage, a career in the family's cloth business, and the indulgence of his adoring parents. All the pleasures of Assisi and the bounty of its surrounding lush vineyards and valleys were his to enjoy.

Then he was captured during a battle with neighboring Perugia, shattering Francis's innocence. A year later, stepping out of prison and into the sunshine, the war veteran saw the world through a lens of anxiety and fear. The Assisi of his childhood, its prosperity and parties, seemed utterly strange. Yet it was Francis who had changed.

One afternoon Francis wandered into an abandoned chapel outside of town. From an icon above the dimly lit altar, the image of Christ crucified spoke to him, spoke *out loud*, saying, "Francis, rebuild my house, which, as you can see, is falling down."[1] Without hesitation, Francis threw himself into the repairs, though he knew nothing of construction work. To purchase building supplies, Francis sold off silks and brocade from the family shop, claiming them for God's purposes as he restored the chapel day by day.

Pietro was furious at his son's thefts and demanded recompense. Pica was perplexed by her son's weird behavior. Newly energized, Francis was determined to continue the project—and he had had it with stifling expectations. He faced down his father in the town piazza, stripped naked in front of everyone, stacked Pietro's precious clothing in a pile before him, and declared God his only father. Francis claimed his freedom to follow God's call anywhere and wherever.

Francis considered the example of Jesus, that traveling teacher who healed the sick, fed the hungry, raised the dead, preached in the fresh air, and declared God's just and beautiful kingdom. Hadn't Jesus upset expectations too? Cut loose from the rules of home, Francis lived each day asking himself, "What would Jesus do?" and then he did it, quite literally.

To Francis, being like Jesus looked like this: tending the disfigured lepers who'd been exiled to remote places; favoring a burlap tunic over the expensive outfits that filled his childhood cupboards; choosing poverty, never touching money, laboring with his hands in exchange for the day's meal; sleeping under the stars; preaching to the birds, talking to crickets, moving worms out of the road to safety, reveling in God's creation along with Brother Sun and Sister Moon.

Francis's joy, humility, and downright foolishness were contagious. Other young men of Assisi (and a young woman named Clare) left their own respectable families to join Francis and create a movement inspired by his exuberant devotion to Christ. Over time, Francis's counterculture settled into Franciscan and Poor Clare religious orders with rules of their own. But even as an old man, Francis refused to compromise for the sake of comfort or convenience. Every day was a fresh invitation to follow Jesus: a lifelong journey of startling challenges and sustaining joys.

## MOTHER KNOWS BEST?

Poor Pica Bernardone! As a parent, I cringe to imagine the scene: the father enraged and the loving mother humiliated, called out by their outrageous son before all the citizens of Assisi. Their rebel son stripping naked in the town square, where he brashly renounces his parents in the name of God despite all they had so generously given him.

She'd only wanted the best for Frenchy. Twelfth-century Italy offered no safety nets, and she knew it; violence, disease, and hunger ravaged the land. The Bernardones were among the lucky few, members of the privileged, rising merchant class who were spared the worst. Why would Francis throw it all away?

I get it, Pica. I want personal and financial security for my own growing children: careers they love, of course, but also the protection of a salary with health insurance, enough to comfortably cover expenses, save for retirement. Sure, we've progressed since the Middle Ages, but as every mother knows, it's still a tough world out there. My kids tell me their dreams, and I hold my breath.

I'll bet Francis's mother looked back and questioned her parenting style. As a teenager, charming Francis had spent lavishly and partied hard, and people murmured that as his parents "were wealthy and loved him very much, they tolerated all these things to avoid upsetting him."[2] When Francis stole valuable merchandise, his dad drew the line and locked him in the cellar. Pica snuck him out, assuring the skeptical neighbors that through God's grace Francis would fall into line. If only she'd practiced tough love, wayward Francis would appreciate all he'd received.

Mothers, we are prone to both blame ourselves and take too much credit. Francis would certainly tell his own story differently. He would speak of the day when he heard, quite audibly, from Christ himself, who called him out of respectability, commerce, and power and into the path of humility, service, and spontaneity. While his parents took his piazza declaration of independence as rebellion, Francis did it as an act of obedience to a higher, greater Parent. He'd found his direction at last.

I wonder if Pica ever came around to her son's radical vocation: to live like Jesus Christ.

Up the slope, in the comfort of her fine townhome, Pica must surely have heard stories of her son's messages of God's generosity, of his joyous singing, his acts of mercy—his strange actions. Other Assisi parents fretted with her as their own kids slipped away from the sureties of merchant society to live free with Francis.

How many saints caused their mothers a world of worry? How tough it is to see the one you love risk their worldly security, health, and safety to do the unexpected, to follow a call. The account of Francis of Assisi unsettles my parent's heart with a challenge: Can I believe that the unexpected, risky path may be the truest path to my child's good future? Might the unexpected way be a new twist in the surprising story that only God can tell?

# TRY THIS

What would Francis and Clare do? Play with that question as you try one or two invitations.

### Family Portraits

> *[Francis] will still be a godly child, through grace.*
>
> —attributed to Pica Bernardone

Francis's mother, Pica, had her own ideas of what a "godly child" would look and act like, yet God's grace would lead her son in a completely different direction.

Take some time to reflect. Close your eyes. Get comfortable. Consider these questions:

- When you were a child, what expectations did your own parents have for you?
- As you've grown, how have you met their expectations?
- When have you done the unexpected?
- What are your hopes for your own future?
- If you are a parent, what has the story of Francis, Pietro, and Pica brought to mind?

Now think of the people who raised you: your parents, grandparents, guardians, or mentors. What prayers might you offer to God on their behalf right now?

### Give It Away

> *Let us love our neighbors as ourselves, with charity and humility. People lose all the material things they leave behind them in this*

*world, but they carry with them the reward of their charity and the alms they give.*

—*Francis of Assisi,* The Letter to the Faithful

Can you freely give to someone else today, with a generosity inspired by Francis? Imagine yourself doing one concrete act of charity, even something small. Consider the spirit of the Italian tradition of *caffè sospeso,* in which someone purchases two coffees but takes only one—paying for the coffee of an unsuspecting stranger. When you have done that act of generosity, pay attention to your thoughts and feelings. Is there an immediate interior reward that you feel when you give your "charity and alms"?

## Flip the Script

What items, tasks, and responsibilities are on your to-do list for this day? Now . . . what would Francis do? Would he walk in the sunshine, help out a neighbor, share the Good News, fix something broken, sing with friends?

Ask yourself:

- What is one unexpected, joyful action I can choose to do today?
- What sacrifice might be required if I am to make that choice?

Write down your "Franciscan" idea (and then do it!).

## Why Do I Do What I Do?

*Our labor here is brief, but the reward is eternal. Do not be disturbed by the clamor of the world, which passes like a shadow. Do not let false delights of a deceptive world deceive you.*

—Clare of Assisi, Letters of Saint Clare to Ermentrude of Bruges

There are many ways to live faithfully in the world; God's callings are varied and dynamic. Are you committed to a simple Franciscan lifestyle? Experiencing professional or material success? Perhaps you have no idea where you're headed, or you are sensing a need to make a change. Clare and Francis of Assisi invite you to consider what's behind your personal ambitions, choices, and career plans. Read the quotation above from Clare one more time. Take five minutes to hear Clare's words as if she were speaking directly to you. Ponder one, two, or even three of these guiding questions:

- Who or what are the three most powerful influences in your life right now?
- Where do your daily efforts give you some sense of enduring purpose?
- What "clamor of the world" or "false delights" might be keeping you from fulfilling your best hopes and values?
- What sense do you have of God's invitation to you?
- If you were truly free to do anything, what would you choose?

# ESCAPE TO THE BEACH

## DOROTHY DAY (1897–1980)

*Dorothy was a New Yorker born and bred,* an urban dweller from her early bohemian days in Greenwich Village to her elder years on the gritty Lower East Side. In the shadow of glittering skyscrapers, corporate wealth, and global power, Dorothy Day's New York was one of soup kitchens, picket lines, political protests, jail time, and communal living.

No worldly ambition drew Dorothy to the city; rather, it was great love that kept her there. "I do not know how to love God except by loving the poor. I do not know how to serve God except by serving the poor," this woman, at once politically radical and theologically orthodox, remarked. "Here, within this great city of nine million people, we must, in this neighborhood, on this street, in this parish, regain a sense of community which is the basis for peace in the world."[1]

For her, community took shape in the Catholic Worker Movement and its houses of hospitality, centers where food, shelter, and clothing were provided freely to anyone in need. There, mercy was no abstraction, since "an extreme of destitution makes all men brothers." One must live with the poor and share in their suffering, Dorothy insisted, and "give up one's privacy, and mental and spiritual comforts as well as physical."[2]

Dorothy Day lived her convictions to the end of her life at age eighty-three. Yet from her spartan combination bedroom-office in the noisy, crowded Catholic Worker Maryhouse among the tenements of Lower Manhattan, she wrote, "I am restless for the beach, not too far away, where I can enjoy the beauties of sunrise over the bay and the sunset." The same Dorothy who labored tirelessly on behalf of the oppressed, who went to prison to oppose war, never stopped longing to be by the bay. Whenever she could make an escape, Dorothy fled to the respite of a "tin roofed fisherman's shack" perched on Raritan Bay, the rough bungalow she had purchased in the 1920s. "One of the joys of Staten Island is that one can get down there after a grueling day in New York, and for thirty-five cents find oneself on a deserted beach," she explained.[3]

As a young woman, Dorothy Day bought the shack on the sea long before the bridge from Brooklyn was built, when Staten Island was a frontier of rural villages and farms. For a time, Dorothy had lived in the simple shelter heated by a driftwood stove with her common-law husband, Forster Batterham, immersed in the natural beauty of the sea and the nourishing company of books, fishermen, horseshoe crabs, and snowy gulls. Dorothy discovered, at last, happiness, peace, wholeness, and, out of the beauty, an unmistakable awakening to God's call.

Dorothy returned to the city with her newborn daughter, Tamar, at the height of the Great Depression, drawn to love and serve the Christ embodied in endless human need. "There I offered up a special prayer," she would recall, "a prayer which came with tears and with anguish, that some way would open up for me to use what talents I possessed for my fellow workers, for the poor."[4] This prayer was answered with a vocation of unflagging sacrifice.

Dorothy Day's Catholic Worker comrades sometimes heard her voice a phrase she attributed to St. Teresa of Ávila: "Life is but a night spent in an uncomfortable inn, crowded together with other wayfarers." Still, they knew her to be a part-time hermit whose exhausting work and life compelled her to slip away to the beach, for space to be by herself, to think and pray and write. One young Staten Island neighbor remembers being told, "Dorothy is here this weekend. If you are playing house, keep off her porch."[5] For those rare restorative days, Dorothy was to be left alone to savor a space all her own, a rickety beach chair, a salty breeze.

Years after Day was buried in Resurrection Cemetery overlooking Raritan Bay, the *New York Times* ran an article, "Dorothy Day's Retreat Is Now a Vacant Lot."[6] Her cottage had been bulldozed by a developer with million-dollar visions that never came to pass. Anyone looking for signs of the place today will find only brush, rubble, some broken tiles, and a discarded tire. These visitors will be left to imagine for themselves the summer evening when Dorothy wrote, "Breakers rolling in on the beach—the air is damp—a flannel nightgown and two blankets are necessary if the windows are open. Opera on the radio—Tannhäuser. The bay is filled with an uncountable number of sailboats."[7]

# WITHIN THE SOUND OF THE WAVES

Each day he spent hours out there in what he called the Prayer Tent. To me, it sure looked like my father was sleeping, his legs sticking out of the old army surplus pup tent, unmoving. Whether praying or sleeping, my dad had certainly earned the rest. He'd survived another rigorous year pastoring a church where he preached at three Sunday services; taught Wednesday night Bible studies; refereed at contentious elders' meetings; and visited, married, buried, counseled, and tended to sweet old ladies, assorted families, needy souls, and more than a few perpetually dissatisfied congregants.

We drove all the way up to Cape Cod each August: two interminable days packed in the station wagon with five squirming kids, Mom, Dad, the dog, the cat, fishing rods, sunscreen, and a minimum of clothes (pro tip: pack clothes in trash bags to save space). Oh, and the pup tent. Before we staggered out, on Cape Cod at last, we always drove straight to the end of the road where Thumpertown Beach and the bay beyond glistened before us. We'd made it.

The cottage we always rented featured three tiny bedrooms, ancient linoleum floors, a screened-in porch, an outdoor cold-water shower—and we loved it. Days at Cape Cod followed a routine. Breakfast, family devotions, cottage cleanup (all hands required), peanut butter sandwiches and Kool-Aid packed, then to the beach for Mom and four kids while one kid stayed back in the shade with a library book (yes, yours truly). My father headed to his familiar spot amid tall, golden grass in the sandy yard shaded by pine trees.

With his Bible, pen, and notebook, Dad crawled into the Prayer Tent and commenced his daily prayer/nap session. No doubt he started with a petition that God would keep all his parishioners alive, at least for the time being; too many funerals had interrupted past vacations. Mornings and afternoons, he took breaks to ride the rickety old bike down to the bay, scanning the horizon for bluefish, whose presence underwater was heralded by diving seagulls. At the end of our vacation, my father would emerge from the pup tent with a completed outline of the next year's sermons and a look of ease on his face.

I can't help but recall Thumpertown Beach when I read Dorothy Day's words, "'In the beginning, God created heaven and earth.' Looking out over the bay, the gulls, the 'paths in the sea,' the tiny ripples stirring a patch of water here and there, the reflections of clouds on the surface—how beautiful it is."[8]

The simple acts of sweeping sand out the door, collecting shells, and plucking flowering weeds to place on the picnic table—both Dorothy and I have done these things, grateful to slip the press of urgent demands, nonstop work, the noise of people, cities, all the rest of it. We've read books and scribbled notes simply for the joy of it. There at the beach, our minds have had space to wander, our eyes free to rest on the last rays of the sun, which we've cheered at its setting in a blaze of orange and chrome, smiling at neighbors who've come on to the sand to see it too.

A few summers back, my husband and I took our kids to Cape Cod, to a house we'd found on Airbnb. Large-screen TV, coffee grinder, Ping-Pong table. Nothing super fancy—but air-conditioning, a dishwasher, and a washer and dryer, naturally. I drove by our old cottage, with its faded cedar shingles, gingham curtains, and flimsy screen door. It looked just the same after all these years, though I wondered if the owner had relented and installed a hot-water heater.

The daylight gleamed through the tall, wild grasses by the clothesline, back where the Prayer Tent had always been. Even in its simplicity, this cottage was luxurious compared to Dorothy Day's rustic fisherman's shack. Yet Dorothy and my father, all of us, really, had once found just what we needed: a brief respite within the sound of the waves.

# TRY THIS

Dorothy Day has lessons to teach on work, life, worship, and rest. Dig deeper with a prompt, maybe two.

### Find Your Own Beach

*One of the joys of Staten Island is that one can get down there after a grueling day in New York, and for thirty-five cents find oneself on a deserted beach.*

—Dorothy Day, "On Pilgrimage"

Are you feeling the pressure of a tough day? A fisherman's shack may not be waiting for you, but think about a getaway within reach, somewhere you could go with your equivalent of thirty-five cents: a bike ride, a walk, or a short drive away. It might be a public park, a hiking path, a walking trail, a hidden garden, a pond—a spot where nature offers some quiet and beauty.

- Can you make a plan to go there today or in the next day or two?
- What tools, toys, or props will you take with you?
- What sights or experiences do you expect to find there?
- As you picture your place, write a few words about it, beginning with Dorothy's words: "One of the joys of [this place] is . . ."

### Workplace Wonderings

That "part-time hermit" Dorothy Day spent her life living, eating, and sleeping in crowded rooms and even jails, marching in street protests, writing books and newspaper columns, leading and serving flawed, even ungrateful, people. Now think about your own everyday physical environment and how it affects you.

- What demands, pressures, and constraints do you experience in the settings and surroundings of your daily life and work?
- What activities, places, or people bring you a sense of relief and respite?
- How do you feel about taking breaks? (Guilty? Conflicted? Trapped? Delighted?) What's behind these feelings?
- What specific change would you like to see in your spaces and rhythms of work and rest?

## Do Like Dorothy

*If we are rushed for time, sow time and we will reap time. Go to church and spend a quiet hour in prayer. You will have more time than ever and your work will get done.*

—Dorothy Day, Long Loneliness

Even on days when Dorothy worked from 7:00 a.m. till midnight, daily morning mass was an essential rhythm of her life. "Sitting . . . in the presence of Jesus . . . warms and gives health to the spirit as the sun gives health to the body," she said.[9] She also pledged to pause in the middle of each day to take "fifteen minutes of absolute quiet, thinking about God and talking to God."[10]

Spirituality was, for Dorothy, not just a vague, personal intention; it required active choice. Dorothy committed to these habits of individual prayer and worship, knowing that they were a source of renewal, even of survival, in her fatigue-filled life.

- Have you ever committed yourself to a spiritual practice that is part of your regular routine, no matter how busy you are? How has that shaped your experience of the rest of your day?

179

- If you were to experiment with a daily spiritual practice, what would you choose and when would it happen?
- Dorothy Day began each morning by walking to her local church to worship with her neighbors. Can you imagine a spiritual practice you might try out in the company of others?
- Dorothy Day paused each midday for individual quiet prayer. Where might you find space for refreshment amidst your own routines?

# TAKE THE LEAD

## MABEL PING-HUA LEE (1896–1966)

*Mounted proudly on a white horse,* Mabel Ping-Hua Lee stood out in the crowd. Like the other women assembled in Washington Square Park, she wore a black hat and a sash emblazoned with the words "Votes for Women." But as the teenager rode out at the head of the 1912 suffragettes' parade, she was the only Chinese girl to be seen among the ten thousand marchers, her presence so notable that it was covered in the pages of the *New York Times.*

In an era when Chinese immigration to the United States was largely banned under the Chinese Exclusion Act, Mabel refused to blend into the background. As a sixteen-year-old agitating for women's rights in America, she set her sights even higher: a place of leadership back home in the infant Republic of China, a nation newly liberated after three thousand years of dynastic rule.

Mabel Lee was born in China but raised in New York City, the brilliant only child of pioneering pastor, missionary, and community leader Rev. Lee To. Mabel rejected the outmoded traditions that had literally crippled her own mother, whose feet were brutally bound when she was a child in the old country, rendering her unable to walk from the family's tenement building on Bayard Street. This Chinese American daughter of a woman whose name is now lost to history would walk into a new future and lead on her own two feet. Mabel declared her aspirations in a speech, saying, "The welfare of China and possibly its very existence as an independent nation depends on rendering tardy justice to its womankind."[1]

Inspired by a bold, transnational vision for democracy based on Christian values of equality, ambitious Mabel Ping-Hua Lee excelled in her public high school and went on to Barnard College. At twenty-five, she completed a PhD in economics from Columbia University, the first Asian American woman to achieve the distinction. As a well-connected, highly trained scholar fluent in English and Chinese, she was eager to exert her influence on the world stage. "Now it is our turn. What are we going to do in answer to the call of duty?" she asked.[2]

Yet not every obstacle gave way. When women gained the right to vote in 1920, Mabel was excluded; as a Chinese person, she would remain barred from US citizenship for another twenty-three years. Nevertheless, Mabel boarded an ocean liner steaming out of New York Harbor, bound for the final stage of her education, a postgraduate fellowship in France. Photographed on the ship's deck with an armful of roses, Dr. Mabel Ping-Hua Lee, at twenty-seven, had no doubt about her calling: "I feel that my life must be devoted to helping my own people in China," she declared. Local media reported that "a position of great trust and signal honor awaits her arrival in China."[3]

What a shock it must have been for Mabel to receive a telegram informing her that her father had died back in New York while negotiating a truce between two warring Chinese gangs known for human trafficking and violent crimes. What was the call of duty now? She opted to return to New York to take over Rev. To's tiny congregation of working-class immigrants. This would be her unforeseen place of leadership.

Dr. Mabel Lee never married, never had children, never moved back to China. Her eminent friends gaining power in the republic wondered what had become of her dreams. Hu Shih, president of Peking University and a Nobel Prize nominee, wrote to her: "Frankly speaking, it is strange that you should spend your life on a thing that is merely a Baptist church in China Town."[4]

For the next forty-one years, Mabel Lee served as the pastor of the First Chinese Baptist Church in Chinatown: an urban neighborhood of eight crowded square blocks, avoided by white Americans who judged Chinese people exotic and threatening. Her parishioners were mostly Chinese men who'd come to America seeking work, forced by the harsh anti-Asian quotas to leave their families behind. She founded the community's Chinese Christian Center, determined to equip struggling immigrants with practical living skills even as she preached a gospel of liberation and hope. She built a legacy that stands today. Manhattan's Chinatown post office was recently named for Mabel Ping-Hua Lee. The church she pastored still opens for worship each Sunday.

Mabel Lee led on her own terms. In the end, sacred duty and a resilient faithfulness would be the measure of her success. She bravely reimagined her dreams in light of all she felt called to do—by God, her family, and her community. "Let us therefore not forget the significance of our work in the mission," she wrote. "It may seem very small, but the influence is very vast. Every little thing we put in counts. Let us rededicate ourselves to our tasks, that every child who comes into the Mission will be made to know Christ. Christianity is the salvation of China, and the salvation of the whole world."[5]

# ACCIDENTAL LEADER?

I don't wear the label "leader" comfortably, and I'm not sure I can say why. Maybe it feels immodest or presumptuous? Years ago, I cofounded Theological Horizons, a campus and community nonprofit, and have been its executive director ever since. I head up a staff, and I oversee funding, budgets, programs, communications, and partnerships. I teach and I speak and I write and I sign the introductory paragraph of each newsletter. I represent Theological Horizons in public and report to a board of directors. I have finally come to say it: yep, I'm a leader.

As the oldest child, I was the responsible sort, called on to babysit, act right, and clear the table. I studied diligently, loved learning, and taught English as a second language after grad school. But if you'd tossed the catalog for the university's School of Leadership and Public Policy to twenty-three-year-old me? I'd have handed it off to one of the smartly dressed guys striding confidently across the lawn, headed out to take on the world.

I attended my own school of leadership without knowing it. The full-time teaching job was interrupted when my husband's doctoral studies took us to another town. I picked up a part-time gig at a nearby college, which gave me time to get Theological Horizons going; it was a side thing, really. The flexibility of a small nonprofit was great during the years our family was growing: one, two, three kids. I put together occasional workshops, raised money for a few scholarships, hosted a lecture here and there, and thought to pray for God's guidance now and then. I loved the theological conversations, took easily to the work's creative demands, found the event planning pleasurable, and managed to file the taxes simply because there was nobody else to do it.

Theological Horizons grew year over year. One friend joined to help part-time. Then a few students needed internships. My own role expanded as I developed new ideas and saw them through. More and more, I was drawn into discussions about the spiritual life. One day, about fifteen years in, as odd as this sounds, I made a trip to Alumni Career Services for the free consultation listed on their website. I sat down in front of the career coach and said, "I happen to be running this organization, but I feel like it happened by accident. What am I *really* cut out to do?" She nodded sagely and slid a thick folder of questionnaires across the desk.

After I'd completed the battery of tests, the Myers-Briggs and Strong Interest Inventory among them, the coach called me in and said, "Karen, I can't tell you what specific job you should be doing, but I do have the results of your personality assessments. They indicate that you are a natural leader; your personality type is common among politicians, coaches, and teachers. People like you are motivated to inspire others. Few things bring you a deeper sense of satisfaction than guiding friends and loved ones toward becoming most truly themselves."

She didn't know me, this woman, and I've never been one for multiple-choice tests. But what she said got me right out of my seat, out the door, and back to work—to *lead* Theological Horizons, to continue the work that, honestly, I do love and is, I daresay, God's calling on my life.

Now I imagine Dr. Mabel Ping-Hua Lee, picture her unlocking the doors of the Chinese Christian Center for the day's lineup of health clinic appointments and for typing, English, and carpentry classes, then heading into her study to write Sunday's sermon. As a driven young woman, Mabel had imagined she'd be back in China, but God's own school of leadership would present her with far different lessons—lessons that would form Mabel into a leader of grit and grace.

# TRY THIS

Truly effective leaders rarely seek larger-than-life icon status. Rather, they are seemingly ordinary people who quietly produce extraordinary results.[6] What makes a leader?

## Role Models

The Bible is filled with stories of leaders—and many are women. In the book of Acts, we meet Tabitha (called Dorcas in Greek), a businesswoman renowned for producing fine clothing. Having embraced the Christian faith, Tabitha emerged as a guiding leader of her church community. In the spirit of the generous Jesus, Tabitha, esteemed by Jews and Greeks alike, gifted her company's garments to everyone in need, no matter their socioeconomic status or ability to repay her.[7] Learn more about Tabitha's story by reading Acts 9.

- In what sphere of life do you act as a leader? What qualities do you bring to that role?
- Where would you like to grow in leadership—in skill, realm, or impact?

## Name Your Little Thing

*Let us therefore not forget the significance of our work in the mission. It may seem very small, but the influence is very vast. Every little thing we put in counts. Let us rededicate ourselves to our tasks.*

—Mabel Ping-Hua Lee, "China's Submerged Half"

- What, do you imagine, allowed Mabel to adapt to the loss of her dreams of leadership in China?

- As you read her words here, do you think of any burden or responsibility, any "little thing," that requires a great deal of your own energy?
- How did you come to carry this "little thing"? Out of duty? Love? Necessity? Guilt? Delight?
- If Mabel were your leadership coach, what might she say to you?
- If the burden is indeed still yours to carry, what would it mean to "rededicate yourself" to the task—and what lasting influence might you have?

# LIFE GOES ON

*The oak tree and I had a unique relationship. I could sit, my back against its trunk, and feel . . . peace. I could reach down in the quiet places of my spirit, take out my bruises and my joys, unfold them, and talk about them. I could talk aloud to the oak tree and know that I was understood. It, too, was part of my reality, like the woods, the night, and the pounding surf, my earliest companions, giving me space.*

—Howard Thurman, With Head and Heart:
The Autobiography of Howard Thurman

*Well,* friend, you've come to the final pages of *Wake Up to Wonder* but not, I trust, to its end. I hope this book has become a sturdy space—like Howard Thurman's childhood oak tree—where you can sit down, lean back, and unfold the joys and bruises of your life in the knowledge that your spirit is safe.

With you, I have been learning that the richest spiritual life is not about achievement. It's about amazement. It's not about labor. It's about play. And it *does* call for curiosity, persistence, and a measure of courage, to wake up in the morning and look, really look, at the universe, near and far.

As you've dipped into some of the personal experiments and spiritual practices offered here, you've surely skipped others. There's no rush. Who knows? If you keep this book near at hand, you may pick it up one morning and find that the moment is exactly right to sketch a leaf, pray the *examen*, march for a cause, or bake Hildegard's Nerve Cookies. (Let me know how those turn out; I'm at karen@theologicalhorizons.org.)

Return to this place to revisit the many spiritual guides you've met: Wangari Maathai, Sophie Scholl, Augustine, Amanda Berry Smith, and all the others. May they become, for you, beloved companions on your pilgrimage into attention, connection, insight, and purpose.

Years and miles removed from his sheltering oak tree, Rev. Dr. Howard Thurman would tell his students that during turbulent times, when we sense a collapse of hope and the press of despair, we must remind ourselves repeatedly that *life goes on*. We easily forget that "the wisdom of life transcends our wisdoms; the purpose of life outlasts our purposes." We fail to affirm "the great and permanent strength of the clean and the commonplace."[1]

But Thurman tells you and me even now, "Let us not be deceived. It is just as important as ever to attend to the little graces by which the dignity of our lives is maintained and sustained. Birds still sing; the stars continue to cast their gentle gleam over the desolation of the battlefields, and the heart is still inspired by the kind word and the gracious deed."[2] There is no need to fear evil, says this man who suffered no illusions about the presence of darkness in the world.

Howard Thurman leaves us with a blessing. He invites us

> to drink in the beauty that is within reach,
> to clothe one's life with simple deeds of kindness,
> to keep alive a sensitiveness to the movement of the spirit
>      of God
> in the quietness of the human heart and in the workings
>      of the human mind—
> this is, as always, the ultimate answer to the great deception.[3]

May it be so.

# ACKNOWLEDGMENTS

*How grateful I am for the everyday miracles of generous friends.*

*For your creative insight and accomplished guidance:* Lauren Winner, Katelyn Beaty and the Brazos team, Sarah Fuentes, Christy Fletcher, Jonathan Merritt, and Sylvie Carr.

*For your generosity and expertise:* James Martin, SJ, of *America*; Dr. Luther E. Smith of Candler School of Theology; Thomas Zimmerman of the Historisches Museum am Strom Hildegard von Bingen; Dr. Gabriele Jancke of the Freie Universität Berlin; Steven Purcell and Gate Davis of Laity Lodge; Amanda Daloisio of *The Catholic Worker*; Justine Hilmer of Lutherhaus Wittenberg, and Tim Tseng, for introducing me to Mabel Ping-hua Lee.

*For your loving care and sustaining presence:* the many partners, students, board members, and friends of Theological Horizons as well as my colleagues Christen Borgman Yates, ElizaBeth Wright, Erin Verham, Kate Harris, Alexa Andrews, Mary-Dryden Maio; the Burning Women: Erica Goldfarb, Jennifer Ackerman, Paige Hornsby, Nita Reigle; Hannah Hicks, Beverly Wispelwey, Larycia Hawkins, Jessicah Duckworth, Roena Clarke, Bob and Myra Marsh, Chuck and Margie Wright, Dan Wright, Beth Anne Melvin, Keith Wright, Christian Wright, and their families.

*And for those to whom I owe the most gratitude:* Charles, Henry, Will and Nan, who know that miracles are everywhere.

# NOTES

**Wake Up**

1. For more thoughts on presence, see Macrina Wiederkehr, *A Tree Full of Angels: Seeing the Holy in the Ordinary* (San Francisco: HarperCollins, 1988).

**Invitation 1  Put Pen to Paper**

1. Henri J. M. Nouwen, *Sabbatical Journey: The Diary of His Final Year* (New York: Crossroad, 1998), 3.

2. Nouwen, *Sabbatical Journey*, 3.

3. Nouwen, *Sabbatical Journey*, 4.

4. Nouwen, *Sabbatical Journey*, 3.

5. Nouwen, *Sabbatical Journey*, 100.

6. Henri J. M. Nouwen, *The Inner Voice of Love* (New York: Image Books, 1998), 115.

7. Nouwen, *Sabbatical Journey*, 5.

8. Nouwen, *Sabbatical Journey*, 5.

9. Nouwen, *Sabbatical Journey*, 6.

10. Henri J. M. Nouwen, *Henri Nouwen: Selected Writings*, Modern Spiritual Masters Series, ed. Robert A. Jonas (Maryknoll, NY: Orbis Books, 1998), 36.

11. Nouwen, *Inner Voice of Love*, 39.

12. Hayley Phelan, "What's All This About Journaling?," *New York Times*, October 25, 2018, https://www.nytimes.com/2018/10/25/style/journaling-benefits.html.

13. Nouwen, *Sabbatical Journey*, 4.

14. Guy Winch, "Why Distinguishing Your Emotions Can Buffer Depression," *Psychology Today*, August 5, 2019, https://www.psychologytoday.com/intl/blog/the-squeaky-wheel/201908/why-distinguishing-your-emotions-can-buffer-depression.

15. Tchiki Davis, "List of Emotions: 271 Emotion Words," Berkeley Well-Being Institute, accessed October 19, 2022, https://www.berkeleywellbeing.com/list-of-emotions.html.

16. Nouwen, *Sabbatical Journey*, 14.

## Invitation 2  Sing Out Loud

1. Martin Luther, *Letters of Spiritual Counsel*, ed. and trans. Theodore G. Tappert (Philadelphia: Westminster Press, 1955), 51.

2. J. Andreas Lowe, "Why Do Lutherans Sing? Lutherans, Music, and the Gospel in the First Century of the Reformation," *Church History* 82, no. 1 (March 2013): 71.

3. Martin Luther, foreword to Georg Rhau's collection "Symphoniae iucundae," accessed Oct. 30, 2022, https://www.eldrbarry.net/mous/saint/luthmusc.htm.

4. Luther, foreword to Georg Rhau's collection "Symphoniae iucundae."

5. Lowe, "Why Do Lutherans Sing?," 71.

6. Lowe, "Why Do Lutherans Sing?," 69–89.

7. Lowe, "Why Do Lutherans Sing?," 73.

8. Lowe, "Why Do Lutherans Sing?," 75.

9. Lowe, "Why Do Lutherans Sing?," 88.

10. Lowe, "Why Do Lutherans Sing?," 89.

11. Anne Fabiny, "Music Can Boost Memory and Mood," Harvard Health Publishing, February 14, 2015, https://www.health.harvard.edu/mind-and-mood/music-can-boost-memory-and-mood.

12. Vox Creative, "You're Not Crazy: That Catchy Song Is Designed to Stick in Your Head," Vox, October 10, 2018, https://www.vox.com/ad/17960634/earworm-song-jingle-advertising-science.

## Invitation 3  Follow Your Breath

1. Thomas Merton, *Thomas Merton, Spiritual Master: The Essential Writings* (Mahwah, NJ: Paulist Press, 1992), 217.

2. See Lynda L. Graybeal and Julia L. Roller, eds., *Connecting with God: A Spiritual Formation Guide*, Renovaré Resources (New York: HarperOne, 2006), 69.

3. James Martin, SJ, "Thomas Merton: Still Controversial," December 10, 2008, https://www.americamagazine.org/faith/2008/12/10/thomas-merton-still-controversial.

4. Thomas Merton, "A Balanced Life of Prayer," The Thomas Merton Center, accessed December 19, 2022, http://merton.org/itms/annual/08/Merton1-21.pdf.

5. Thomas Merton, *The Courage for Truth: The Letters of Thomas Merton to Writers*, ed. Christine M. Bochen (New York: Farrar, Straus & Giroux, 1993), 225.

6. Thomas Merton, *Thomas Merton: Essential Writings*, ed. Robert Ellsberg (Maryknoll, NY: Orbis Books, 2008), 83.

7. Melissa Madeson, "12+ Breathing Exercises for Managing Anxiety," Positive Psychology.com, December 31, 2021, https://positivepsychology.com/breathing-exercises.

8. Madeson, "12+ Breathing Exercises."

9. Madeson, "12+ Breathing Exercises."

10. Merton, "A Balanced Life of Prayer."

## Invitation 4  Fuel Up

1. Sam O'Brien, "Eat Like a Medieval Saint With Her Recipe for 'Cookies of Joy,'" Atlas Obscura, September 20, 2021, https://www.atlasobscura.com/articles /medieval-cookie-recipe.

2. Hildegard von Bingen, *Physica, The Complete English Translation of Her Classic Work on Health and Healing*, trans. Priscilla Throop (Rochester, VT: Healing Arts Press, 1998), 13.

3. Hildegard von Bingen, *Physica*, 21.

4. Hildegard von Bingen, *Physica*, 9.

5. Hildegard von Bingen, *St. Hildegard of Bingen—Doctor of the Church: A Spiritual Reader*, ed. Carmen Acevedo Butcher (Brewster, MA: Paraclete, 2013), epigraph.

6. Hildegard von Bingen, *Illuminations of Hildegard of Bingen*, ed. Matthew Fox (Rochester, VT: Inner Traditions, 2002), xvi.

7. On fennel as a cure for headache, see Hildegard von Bingen, *Physica*, 40.

8. Hildegard von Bingen, *Physica*, 13.

9. Uma Naidoo, *This Is Your Brain on Food* (New York: Little, Brown–Spark, 2020), 251.

10. "The Biofloral Laboratory," Biofloral Organic Herbal Remedies, accessed October 20, 2022, https://www.biofloral.fr/en/content/27-the-biofloral -laboratory.

11. "Fruits and Vegetables Serving Sizes Infographic," American Heart Association, accessed Oct. 20, 2022, https://www.heart.org/en/healthy-living /healthy-eating/add-color/fruits-and-vegetables-serving-sizes.

12. Hildegard von Bingen, *Physica*, xxv.

13. Adin Smith, "The Immune Benefits of Circumin," Nordic Naturals, accessed Oct. 20, 2022, https://www.nordic.com/healthy-science/the-immune -benefits-of-curcumin.

14. Naidoo, *This Is Your Brain on Food*, 251.

## Invitation 5  Keep On Walking

1. Margery Kempe, *The Book of Margery Kempe*, trans. John Skinner (New York: Image, Doubleday, 1998), 46, 58.

2. Kempe, *Book of Margery Kempe*, 116.

3. Kempe, *Book of Margery Kempe*, 56.

4. Kempe, *Book of Margery Kempe*, 58.

5. Kempe, *Book of Margery Kempe*, 38.

6. Kempe, *Book of Margery Kempe*, 327.

7. Here I borrow from Jean-Jacques Rousseau, who wrote, "There is something about walking which stimulates and enlivens my thoughts. When I stay in one place I can hardly think at all; my body has to be on the move to set my mind going." *The Confessions of Jean-Jacques Rousseau*, trans. J. M. Cohen (New York: Penguin Books, 1953), 158.

8. Kempe, *Book of Margery Kempe*, 116.

9. *The Belles Heures of Jean de Berry*, as quoted in Jean Sorabella, "Pilgrimage in Medieval Europe," The Met, April 2011, https://www.metmuseum.org/toah/hd/pilg/hd_pilg.htm.

## Invitation 6  Plant a Tree

1. Wangari Maathai, *Unbowed* (New York: Anchor Books, 2007), 44.

2. Maathai, *Unbowed*, 175.

3. Maathai, *Unbowed*, 121–22.

4. Maathai, *Unbowed*, 124.

5. Maathai, *Unbowed*, 125.

6. Maathai, *Unbowed*, 287.

7. Maathai, *Unbowed*, 173.

8. Maathai, *Unbowed*, 203.

9. Maathai, *Unbowed*, 292–93.

10. Bob Abernethy interview with Wangari Maathai, PBS Religion & Ethics Newsweekly, November 9, 2007, https://www.pbs.org/wnet/religionandethics/2007/11/09/november-9-2007-wangari-maathai/4544.

11. Bob Abernethy interview with Wangari Maathai.

12. Maathai, *Unbowed*, 293.

13. Maathai, *Unbowed*, 293.

14. Maathai, *Unbowed*, 307.

15. Learn more about the Nature Conservancy's Plant a Billion Trees campaign and consider donating at www.nature.org/en-us/get-involved/how-to-help/plant-a-billion/.

## Invitation 7  Say Thank You

1. Dictionary of National Biography, s.v. "Caedmon," December 28, 2020, https://en.wikisource.org/wiki/Dictionary_of_National_Biography,_1885-1900/C%C3%A6dmon.

2. Dictionary of National Biography, s.v. "Caedmon."

3. Gary Moon, *Becoming Dallas Willard* (Downers Grove, IL: IVP Books, 2018), 240.

4. Dallas Willard, *The Spirit of the Disciplines* (San Francisco: Harper & Row, 1988), 179.

5. Dallas Willard, "Thou Shalt Celebrate," Renovaré, December 1987, https://renovare.org/articles/thou-shalt-celebrate.

6. See more on Robert Emmons's view of gratitude in Emma Green, "Gratitude without God," *The Atlantic*, November 26, 2014, https://www.theatlantic .com/health/archive/2014/11/the-phenomenology-of-gratitude/383174/.

### Invitation 8  Pray Your Anything

1. Amanda Berry Smith, *An Autobiography: The Story of the Lord's Dealings with Mrs. Amanda Berry Smith the Colored Evangelist* (New York: Oxford University Press, 1988), 47.

2. Smith, *Autobiography*, 47.

3. Amanda Berry Smith, quoted in Jamie Janosz, "Freed for Evangelism: The Story of Former Slave Amanda Berry Smith," *Christianity Today*, March 26, 2014, https://www.christianitytoday.com/ct/2014/march-web-only/freed -for-evangelism-story-of-former-slave-amanda-berry-smi.html.

4. Smith, *Autobiography*, 147, 148.

5. Smith, *Autobiography*, 505, 506.

6. Shane Claiborne, Jonathan Wilson-Hartgrove, and Enuma Okoro, *Common Prayer: A Liturgy for Ordinary Radicals* (Grand Rapids: Zondervan, 2010).

7. Smith, *Autobiography*, 46, 80.

8. Anne Lamott, *Help, Thanks, Wow: The Three Essential Prayers* (New York: Penguin, 2012).

9. Smith, *Autobiography*, 78.

10. Lamott, *Help, Thanks, Wow*, 1.

11. This and other African prayers can be found in Desmond Tutu, *An African Prayer Book* (New York: Doubleday, 1995). Some examples can be found at https://www.dailyom.com/cgi-bin/display/librarydisplay.cgi?lid=461.

12. Flannery O'Connor, *A Prayer Journal* (New York: Farrar, Straus & Giroux, 2013), 3–4. Copyright © 2013 by the Mary Flannery O'Connor Charitable Trust. Reprinted by permission of Farrar, Straus and Giroux. All rights reserved. United Kingdom copyright © 2013 by the Mary Flannery O'Connor Charitable Trust via Harold Matson–Ben Camardi, Inc. All rights reserved.

13. Thomas Merton, *Thoughts in Solitude* (New York: Farrar, Straus & Giroux, 1956), 79. Copyright © 1958 by the Abbey of Our Lady of Gethsemani. Copyright renewed 1986 by the Trustees of the Thomas Merton Legacy Trust. Reprinted by permission of Farrar, Straus and Giroux. All rights reserved. United Kingdom copyright © 1956, 1958 by The Abbey of Our Lady of Gethsemane, renewed. Reprinted by permission of Curtis Brown, Ltd. All rights reserved.

14. We conclude each Theological Horizons event with this blessing.

### Invitation 9  Ask Better Questions

1. Augustine, *The Confessions of Saint Augustine*, ed. Hal M. Helms (Brewster, MA: Paraclete, 2010), 3, adapted.

2. Justin Taylor, "How Augustine Wrote So Many Books," The Gospel Coalition, June 12, 2018, https://www.thegospelcoalition.org/blogs/evangelical-history/augustine-wrote-many-books/.

3. Augustine, *The Confessions*, trans. Henry Chadwick (Oxford: Oxford University Press, 2008), 194, adapted.

4. This idea is taken from Nathan Eric Dickman, *Using Questions to Think: How to Develop Skills in Critical Understanding and Reasoning* (New York: Bloomsbury Academic, 2021).

5. Augustine, *Confessions* (Chadwick), 71, adapted.

6. Augustine, *Confessions* (Chadwick), 145.

7. Augustine, *Confessions* (Helms), 166.

8. Charles T. Mathewes, "The Liberation of Questioning in Augustine's Confessions," *Journal of the American Academy of Religion* 70, no. 3 (2002), https://www.jstor.org/stable/1466523.

9. Daniel Jones, "The 36 Questions That Lead to Love," *New York Times*, January 9, 2015, https://www.nytimes.com/2015/01/09/style/no-37-big-wedding-or-small.html.

10. Jones, "36 Questions That Lead to Love."

11. Augustine, "A Collection of Prayers" in Jeremy Taylor, *The Westminster Collection of Christian Prayer* (Louisville: Presbyterian Publishing, 2004), 131.

12. Augustine, *Confessions* (Chadwick), 3.

13. See Paul Tillich, *Dynamics of Faith* (New York: HarperCollins, 2001), 25.

14. Mathewes, "The Liberation of Questioning."

15. Jones, "36 Questions That Lead to Love."

**Invitation 10  Look to See**

1. "About Miriam," interview with Miriam Rockness, WordPress.com, accessed Nov. 6, 2022, https://ililiastrotter.wordpress.com/about-miriam/.

2. Lilias Trotter, *Parables of the Cross* (1895; repr., Mount Dora, FL: Lilias Trotter Legacy, 2021), 5.

3. "Biography of Lilias Trotter," Lilias Trotter Legacy, 2020, https://liliastrotter.com/about/.

4. See Miriam H. Rockness, "A Way of Seeing," WordPress.com, September 6, 2014, https://ililiastrotter.wordpress.com/2014/09/12/a-way-of-seeing/.

5. See Rockness, "A Way of Seeing."

6. See Eve M. Kahn, "A Renewed Spotlight on Two Women Artists," *New York Times*, May 19, 2016, https://www.nytimes.com/2016/05/20/arts/design/a-renewed-spotlight-on-two-women-artists.html.

7. See Rockness, "A Way of Seeing."

8. See Miriam H. Rockness, "Mountain Lesson," WordPress.com, August 11, 2012, https://ililiastrotter.wordpress.com/2012/08/11/mountain-lesson/.

9. "Going Deeper: Tools for Learning," Lilias Trotter Legacy, 2020, https://liliastrotter.com/resources/tools-for-learning/.

10. "Quotes from the Writings of Lilias Trotter," Lilias Trotter Legacy, 2020, https://liliastrotter.com/quotes/.

11. "Quotes from the Writings of Lilias Trotter."

### Invitation 11  Raise Your Voice

1. Hamer, quoted in Charles Marsh, *God's Long Summer: Stories of Faith and Civil Rights* (Princeton: Princeton University Press, 1997), 12.

2. Hamer, quoted in Marsh, *God's Long Summer*, 25.

3. Hamer, quoted in Marsh, *God's Long Summer*, 33.

4. Larycia Hawkins, Facebook post, December 13, 2015, https://www.facebook.com/larycia/posts/10153331120918481.

5. Ruth Graham, "The Professor Who Wore a Hijab in Solidarity—Then Lost Her Job," *New York Times Magazine*, October 13, 2016, https://www.nytimes.com/2016/10/16/magazine/the-professor-wore-a-hijab-in-solidarity-then-lost-her-job.html.

6. Mahatma K. Gandhi, "For Shame," Gandhian Institutions–Bombay Sarvodaya Mandal & Gandhi Research Foundation, accessed November 6, 2022, https://www.mkgandhi.org/mynonviolence/chap84.htm.

7. This film is available through various media outlets. Information on the film is available at https://samegodfilm.com.

8. "'Songs of Salvation': Remembering Fannie Lou Hamer's Music," NPR, July 18, 2015, https://www.npr.org/2015/07/18/423605660/songs-of-salvation-remembering-fannie-lou-hamers-music. Audio recordings of Fannie Lou Hamer are available for purchase at https://folkways.si.edu/fannie-lou-hamer/songs-my-mother-taught-me/african-american-gospel-struggle-protest/music/album/smithsonian.

### Invitation 12  Embrace Alone

1. St. Patrick, *The Confession of Saint Patrick and Letter to Coroticus*, trans. John Skinner (New York: Doubleday, 1998), ix.

2. St. Patrick, "Confession," Logos Virtual Library, accessed November 6, 2022, https://www.logoslibrary.org/patrick/confession.html.

3. *Online Entymology Dictionary*, s.v. "alone," accessed December 16, 2022, https://www.etymonline.com/word/alone.

4. Børge Ousland, *Alone to the North Pole* (Oslo, Norway: J. W. Cappeleans, 1994), 25.

5. Nadia Whitehead, "People Would Rather Be Electrically Shocked Than Left Alone with Their Thoughts," *Science*, July 3, 2014, https://www.science.org/content/article/people-would-rather-be-electrically-shocked-left-alone-their-thoughts.

6. Henri J. M. Nouwen, *Devotional Classics: Selected Readings for Individuals and Groups*, ed. Richard J. Foster and James Bryan Smith, rev. ed. (New York: HarperCollins, 2005), 82.

7. I borrow the phrase "tonic of the wilderness" from Henry David Thoreau, *Walden: Or, Life in the Woods*, (1846, repr., New York: New American Library, 1960), 142.

8. Tanya Davis, "How to Be Alone," YouTube video by Andrea Dorfman, July 28, 2010, https://www.youtube.com/watch?v=k7X7sZzSXYs&ab_channel=Andrea Dorfman.

9. Jessica Stillman, "The Incredible Brain Benefits of Silence," Inc.com, July 19, 2016, https://www.inc.com/jessica-stillman/science-silence-is-really-good -for-you.html.

### Invitation 13  Review the News

1. See Richard Hanser, *A Noble Treason: The Story of Sophie Scholl and the White Rose Revolt against Hitler vs the Revolt of the Munich Students against Hitler* (San Francisco: Ignatius Press, 2012), 44.

2. Karen Wright Marsh, *Vintage Saints and Sinners: 25 Christians Who Transformed My Faith* (Downers Grove, IL: InterVarsity, 2017), 178.

3. See Annette Dumbach and Jud Newborn, *Sophie Scholl and the White Rose* (London: OneWorld, 2018), 20.

4. See Karen Wright Marsh, "To Knock a Chip out of the Wall: Sophie Scholl," *Comment*, December 1, 2017, https://comment.org/to-knock-a-chip-out-of-the -wall-sophie-scholl/.

5. "Leaflets of the White Rose," Weisse Rose Stiftung e.V., 2017, https://www .weisse-rose-stiftung.de/white-rose-resistance-group/leaflets-of-the-white-rose/.

6. Dumbach and Newborn, *Sophie Scholl and the White Rose*, 48.

7. Hans Scholl in "'Es lebe die Freiheit': Als die Geschwister Scholl ihren Tod durch die Guillotine fanden," accessed Nov. 6, 2022, https://www.diepresse .com/5376292/es-lebe-die-freiheit-als-die-geschwister-scholl-ihren-tod-durch -die-guillotine-fanden.

8. A facsimile of "Freiheit" in Sophie's script can be seen at https://www .weisse-rose-stiftung.de/white-rose-resistance-group/.

9. "How the News Changes the Way We Think and Behave," Association for Psychological Science, May 20, 2020, https://www.psychologicalscience.org /news/how-the-news-changes-the-way-we-think-and-behave.html.

10. "How the News Changes the Way We Think and Behave."

11. Helen Coster, "Number of Jailed Journalists Reached Global High in 2021, at Least 24 Killed for Their Coverage," December 9, 2021, https://www.reuters .com/world/china/number-jailed-journalists-reached-global-high-2021-least -24-killed-their-2021-12-09/.

### Invitation 14  Take a Pause

1. Howard Thurman, *With Head and Heart: The Autobiography of Howard Thurman* (New York: Harcourt, Brace, Jovanovich, 1979), 7.

200

2. Thurman, *With Head and Heart*, 21.

3. Howard Thurman, *Howard Thurman: Essential Writings*, ed. Luther E. Smith (Maryknoll, NY: Orbis Books, 2006), 15.

4. Thurman, *Essential Writings*, 118.

5. Thurman, *Essential Writings*, 118.

6. Thurman, *Essential Writings*, 60, 61.

7. Thurman, *Essential Writings*, 60.

8. Howard Thurman, *A Strange Freedom: The Best of Howard Thurman on Religious Experience and Public Life* (Boston: Beacon, 2014), 90.

9. James Hamblin and Katherine Wells, interview with Tricia Hersey, *Social Distance* podcast, April 30, 2020, https://www.theatlantic.com/health/archive/2020/04/you-are-worthy-of-sleep/610996/.

10. Elizabeth Pennisi, "The Simplest of Slumbers," *Science*, October 28, 2021, https://www.science.org/content/article/if-alive-sleeps-brainless-creatures-shed-light-why-we-slumber.

11. Thurman, *With Head and Heart*, 7.

12. Thurman, *Essential Writings*, 61.

13. Tricia Hersey, "Rest Is Anything That Connects Your Mind and Body," The Nap Ministry, February 21, 2022, https://thenapministry.wordpress.com/2022/02/21/rest-is-anything-that-connects-your-mind-and-body/. Read more in her book, *Rest Is Resistance: A Manifesto* (Boston: Little, Brown, 2022).

14. Jonathan Bender, "Want to Sleep Faster? Try Taking a Bath One Hour before Bedtime," Sleep.com, March 29, 2022, https://www.sleep.com/sleep-health/benefits-of-a-hot-bath.

15. Howard Thurman, *Meditations of the Heart* (Boston: Beacon, 1953), 83–84.

## Invitation 15  Wander through Scripture

1. Keith J. White, "Jesus Was Her Guru," Christian History Institute, accessed December 16, 2022, https://www.christianitytoday.com/history/issues/issue-87/jesus-was-her-guru.html.

2. Meera Kosambi, *Pandita Ramabai: Life and Landmark Writings* (London: Taylor & Francis, 2016), 272.

3. Kosambi, *Pandita Ramabai*, 272, 273.

4. Kosambi, *Pandita Ramabai*, 274.

## Invitation 16  Surround Yourself with Beauty

1. Sidney Harrison Griffith, *Faith Adoring the Mystery: Reading the Bible with St. Ephraim the Syrian* (Milwaukee: Marquette University Press, 1997), 22.

2. John Wesley, *The Works of the Rev. John Wesley, A.M.* (London: John Mason, 1829), 48.

3. St. Ephrem, *Ephrem the Syrian: Hymns*, trans. Kathleen E. McVey, Classics of Western Spirituality (Mahwah, NJ: Paulist Press, 1989), 203.

4. Marianne Wright, "The Coming Light: Hymns of St. Ephrem the Syrian" *Plough*, December 12, 2018, https://www.plough.com/en/topics/culture/music/the-coming-light.

5. These quotations are from "St. Ephrem's Hymn to the Light." The hymn can be heard on YouTube, posted by Christian Maronite, December 29, 2012, https://www.youtube.com/watch?v=oTcsS-CBEa8.

6. "St. Ephrem's Hymn to the Light."

7. "St. Ephrem's Hymn to the Light."

8. John Rutter, comp., "Requiem: Lux Aeterna," from *Visions and Rutter Requiem* (Collegium Records, 2016).

9. St. Ephrem, *Ephrem the Syrian: Hymns*, 47.

## Invitation 17 Replay the Day

1. Paul Van Dyke, *Ignatius of Loyola: The Founder of the Jesuits* (New York: Scribner's Sons, 1926), 31.

2. "St. Ignatius: The Man Who Changed the World," Travelling Steps, April 16, 2021, https://travelingsteps.es/saint-ignatius-created-the-jesuits-and-changed-the-world-for-ever.

3. See David L. Fleming, *The Spiritual Exercises of Saint Ignatius: A Literal Translation and Contemporary Reading* (St. Louis: Institute of Jesuit Sources, 1991), 23.

4. See James Martin, *The Jesuit Guide to (Almost) Everything* (New York: HarperCollins, 2010), 18.

5. Read about the *examen* in Fleming, *Spiritual Exercises of St. Ignatius*, 23. For an extended treatment, see Timothy M. Gallagher, *The Examen Prayer: Ignatian Wisdom for Our Lives Today* (New York: Crossroad, 2006).

6. Adapted from Martin, *Jesuit Guide to (Almost) Everything*, and Margaret Silf, *Inner Compass: An Invitation to Ignatian Spirituality* (Chicago: Loyola, 1999).

## Invitation 18 Design a Life

1. For a glimpse into Benedictine monastic life, read Jonathan Malesic, "Taming the Demon: How Desert Monks Put Work in Its Place," *Commonweal*, February 2, 2019, https://www.commonwealmagazine.org/taming-demon.

2. St. Benedict of Nursia, *The Rule of Saint Benedict: A Contemporary Paraphrase*, ed. Jonathan Wilson-Hartgrove (Brewster, MA: Paraclete, 2012), vii.

3. Pope Gregory, *Life and Miracles of St. Benedict* (Collegeville, MN: Liturgical Press, 1980), 67–69.

4. These lines are from MacBeth's famous soliloquy in Act 5 of Shakespeare's play named after this protagonist.

5. Oliver Burkeman, "On Time Management: Breaking Down the Façade of Productivity," July 26, 2022, https://findingmastery.net/oliver-burkeman/.

6. Robert Benson, *A Good Life: Benedict's Guide to Everyday Joy* (Brewster, MA: Paraclete, 2004), 78.

7. The website https://pray-as-you-go.org offers brief daily meditations.

8. From *The Book of Common Prayer* (Oxford: Oxford University Press, 1979), 461.

9. St. Benedict (Abbot of Montecassino), *The Rule of Saint Benedict*, ed. Timothy Fry (New York: Knopf, 1998), 4.

**Invitation 19  Choose Your Intention**

1. C. J. Snyder, "Brother Lawrence," *Engage*, July 14, 2017, https://engagemaga zine.net/starting-blog/heroes/brother-lawrence/.

2. Brother Lawrence, *Practicing the Presence of God*, trans. Robert J. Edmonson (Brewster, MA: Paraclete, 2007), 85.

3. Brother Lawrence, *Practicing the Presence of God*, 20.

4. Brother Lawrence, *Practicing the Presence of God*, 21.

5. Brother Lawrence, *Practicing the Presence of God*, 82, 136.

6. Joan Chittister, "Foreword," in Mary Lou Kownacki, *The Sacred in the Simple: Making Mantras Part of Christian Living* (Liguori, MO: Liguori, 1995), 2.

7. Brother Lawrence, *Practicing the Presence of God*, 72, 90.

8. Brother Lawrence, *Practicing the Presence of God*, 22.

9. Lawrence Kushner, *The Book of Words: Talking Spiritual Life, Living Spiritual Talk* (Woodstock, VT: Longhill, 1993), 20.

10. Michael Gray Baughan, *E. E. Cummings*, Bloom's Major Poets (Broomall, PA: Haights Cross, 2003), 87.

11. Toni Morrison, "James Baldwin: His Voice Remembered, Life in His Language," *New York Times*, accessed Nov. 10, 2022, https://www.nytimes.com/1987/12/20/books/james-baldwin-his-voice-remembered-life-in-his-language.html.

12. Thich Nhat Hanh, *Stepping into Freedom: An Introduction to Buddhist Monastic Training* (Berkeley: Parallax, 1997), 2.

13. Brother Lawrence, *Practicing the Presence of God*, 21.

14. This is the theme of B. J. Fogg, *Tiny Habits* (New York: Houghton Mifflin Harcourt, 2019).

15. Adapted from Brother Lawrence, *Practicing the Presence of God*.

**Invitation 20  Do the Unexpected**

1. Augustine Thompson, *Francis of Assisi: A New Biography* (Ithaca, NY: Cornell University Press, 2012), 7.

2. Donald Spoto, *Reluctant Saint: The Life of Francis of Assisi* (New York: Viking, 2002), 25.

**Invitation 21  Escape to the Beach**

1. Dorothy Day, "On Pilgrimage–October 1950," Catholic Worker Movement, accessed December 16, 2022, https://catholicworker.org/615-html/.

2. Dorothy Day, *The Long Loneliness* (New York: HarperCollins, 1952), 215, 214.

3. David Allen, "'Down Here Near the End of Staten Island': Dorothy Day on the Beach and on the Page," Gotham Center for New York City History, August 6, 2020, https://www.gothamcenter.org/blog/down-here-near-the-end-of-staten -island-dorothy-day-on-the-beach-and-on-the-page.

4. Dorothy Day, "On Pilgrimage–December 1948," Catholic Worker Movement, accessed December 16, 2022, https://catholicworker.org/486-html/.

5. Allen, "Down Here Near the End of Staten Island."

6. Matt A. V. Chaban, "Dorothy Day's Retreat Is Now a Vacant Lot, but a Bid to Protect It Survives," *New York Times*, October 27, 2015, https://www.ny times.com/2015/10/27/nyregion/dorothy-days-retreat-is-now-a-vacant-lot-but -a-bid-to-protect-it-survives.html.

7. Dorothy Day, "On Pilgrimage–July/August 1978, Catholic Worker Movement, accessed December 16, 2022, https://catholicworker.org/590-html/.

8. See Allen, "Down Here Near the End of Staten Island."

9. Jessie Bazan, "Dorothy Day: The Contemplative Catholic Worker," *Obsculta* 10, no 1 (May 17, 2017), https://digitalcommons.csbsju.edu/cgi/viewcontent.cgi? article=1172&context=obsculta.

10. Dorothy Day, *The Duty of Delight: The Diaries of Dorothy Day*, ed. Robert Ellsberg (New York: Crown Publishing, 2011), 17.

**Invitation 22  Take the Lead**

1. Jia Lynn Yang, "Overlooked No More: Mabel Ping-Hua Lee, Suffragette with a Distinction," *New York Times*, September 19, 2020, https://www.nytimes .com/2020/09/19/obituaries/mabel-ping-hua-lee-overlooked.html.

2. Mabel Ping Hua Lee, "China's Submerged Half," in Tim Tseng, "Asian American Legacy: Dr. Mabel Lee," accessed December 16, 2022, WordPress .com, https://timtsengdotnet.files.wordpress.com/2013/12/mabel-lee-speech -china_s-submerged.pdf.

3. Lee, "China's Submerged Half."

4. Lee, "China's Submerged Half."

5. Tim Tseng, "Chinatown's Suffragist, Pastor and Community Organizer," *Christianity Today*, June 16, 2017, https://www.christianitytoday.com/history /2017/june/mabel-lee-chinatown-suffragist-pastor-community-organizer.html.

6. Jim Collins, *Good to Great: Why Some Companies Make the Leap . . . and Others Don't* (New York: HarperCollins, 2001), 12.

7. Read a profile of Tabitha, along with other biblical and early Christian women, at knowyourmothers.com.

**Life Goes On**

1. Howard Thurman, *Meditations of the Heart* (Boston: Beacon, 1981), 110.

2. Thurman, *Meditations of the Heart*, 110.

3. Thurman, *Meditations of the Heart*, 111.

**Karen Wright Marsh** is the founding director of Theological Horizons, a ministry at the University of Virginia that hosts lectures, spiritual studies, dialogues, and mentoring initiatives. She is the author of *Vintage Saints and Sinners: 25 Christians Who Transformed My Faith*, which was named an *Outreach* Resource of the Year, a Logos Booksellers Book of the Year, and a *Foreword* INDIES finalist. Karen holds a degree in philosophy from Wheaton College and a degree in linguistics from the University of Virginia. She lives with her professor husband, Charles Marsh, at the Bonhoeffer House in Charlottesville, Virginia.